Just A Misunderstanding

The Missing Keys to Financial Stability

Robin Walker

BOOK DESCRIPTION

The following text is not about how to get rich necessarily, but rather a guide to building the foundation of wealth for yourself and generations to come. In this book, you will discover the meaning of true wealth and how to seal financial leaks to create your dream future and finally afford the lifestyle you wish. Keep in mind that wealth and poverty alike are a state of mind. Thoughts are very powerful within the financial process.

Although a world of resources exists today to teach you how to generate money; from podcasts to blogs to books, this book throws all the 'get rich quick' B.S. to the curb. First, build the foundation for wealth, then climb up your ladder.

I hope you will enjoy this book as much as I have enjoyed putting it together for you!

Table of Contents

Introduction..*1*

My Story..*3*...

Chapter 1

    Poverty is a State of Mind..*5*

Chapter 2

    Thoughts Equals Outcome...................................... *14*

Chapter 3

    Values Alignment..*25*

Chapter 4

    What About the Money *33*

Chapter 5

    Emotional Charge *41*

Chapter 6

    An Intentional Life..*50*

Chapter 7

    Wealth Stability..*58*

Chapter 8

    Investing in Yourself *70*

Chapter 9

    Spending Plan..*81*

Chapter 10

    Leverage *91*

Conclusion..*101*

References..*106*

INTRODUCTION

Hello readers! I am so delighted that you have chosen to educate yourself financially and have found a way to make your dream lifestyle become your reality with some time and effort. Throughout the contents of this book, you will be able to build a foundation for wealth like never before and truly understand the reasoning for habits that are holding you back. I also hope to introduce you to a version of yourself that you always wished to become. Someone who is knowledgeable, self-aware, and financially secure. The road to peace of mind and financial security begins for the person at the individual level before it ever reaches finances. Becoming a better you will mean you are bettering your life and in turn, your lifestyle. It is a long journey and I am happy to be the crutch you need to begin.

While everyone is eager to grasp the secret to becoming rich and wealthy overnight, no such formula exists. The road to becoming financially stable and comfortable is one with many twists and turns and unexpected exercises to try and master. Everything within this text begins and ends with you, and your dedication on the topic. There is no one exercise and no one chapter is dedicated to helping you become a millionaire but it is intended that you learn better how to navigate your finances when you have finished this book. Breaking the cycle of not being or having enough is the toughest for the first person who decides to take a stand but does absolute wonders for one's legacy.

This book will be more direct and to-the-point in the sense that you need more than just money and motivation to become the person you want to be. A wealthier and better version of yourself does not depend on your income or the way you invest your money. It is all dependent on the mindset, emotional charge, and the grounding of the person you are right now. Your future is completely dictated by the person you are today, and I hope to open your mind up to new experiences and horizons in order to reach places you have never before.

In this book full of examples, ideas and exercises, you can be expected to be introduced to a world full of secrets within you. Financial stability needs a stable mind to come home to. Keeping yourself peaceful and aware is another step closer to the ideal you. Financial worries will cease to exist once you are able to create your budgets and spending plan accordingly.

And so, I hope to connect you with your inner self further and guide you on a path of self-love, self-awareness, great habits, and a wealthy mindset. Be sure to interact well with the parts of the book that require you to complete an activity.

MY STORY

My name is Robin Walker. I was inspired to become a Financial Educator because when I was only 18 years old I received an unexpected inheritance of two boys and two girls. My mom passed away and left behind no savings. My dad did all he could do and that was to work to pay the endless cycle of bills. Finally, I made the hard decision and decided to not attend college in order to raise my siblings. I finally landed a job to help with household finances, and although my father and I both worked, it still was not enough and we lived paycheck to paycheck. We were working so hard with nothing to show for or have peace of mind in case of emergencies.

As the years went on, and my siblings began growing up, they were able to begin taking care of each other and themselves. I eventually got married and decided to start my own family. My partner and I were both blessed with good-paying jobs, but still noticed the pattern of living paycheck to paycheck with no life insurance and little savings. We also were making no investments for our future and had limited assets. Our situation was a slight improvement from that of my parents', but essentially, we were victims to the same habits.

Fast forward to 2015, I decided to make a career change and obtain a license to pursue a career as a real estate agent. In my career, I was able to help many people obtain homeownership, but there were some cases that did not allow for some to buy a home. This was not enough for me. I wanted to help every client with their dreams of becoming homeowners, and so, I got to work. I put in the time to do some research and discovered the same problem my parents faced, some of my clients and now I was going through; financial illiteracy. Although we thought we had it figured out, we were never fully educated on financial matters.

This discovery took me on a journey of self-awareness and development. I studied myself and found that many of my beliefs, habits, and values were countering my dream lifestyle. Additionally, I realized that my life, and in turn my finances, are directly connected to my children.

I knew that these habits needed to change at once. Not just for myself and my family, but for anyone looking to break the cycle and take control over their life. And so, with another effort to pursue a different career path, I became a lifestyle strategist and certified financial educator to help promote financial literacy and hold my clients accountable for personal goals. Financial illiteracy has been and will continue to be passed down from generation to generation. We need to break the cycle, and do so, today!

CHAPTER 1

Poverty is a State of Mind

The power of the mind is truly remarkable and a notable factor that affects any and all aspects of your life- even when you think otherwise. Do not take manifestation and its ability to make things happen lightly. Always remember that how you think is how you carry yourself, and how you carry yourself affects your lifestyle. Your mindset sets the precedent for your life. Even the financial bits and pieces.

It may seem corny, but true wealth is in the mind. Wealth can be an abundance of love to give and to receive or it can be having enough to feed your stomach for the day, dealer's choice. Perspective is king and no two perspectives have to be identical. Just like how a real designer bag might announce wealth for some while screaming basic for others. First, clear your thoughts and figure out-for yourself-what it means to be wealthy. Will you consider yourself wealthy when you have your 401k saved up? Or will you claim wealth when you own five different properties? It is important to figure these things out within your mindset to determine how you will go about becoming wealthy- in your own way.

A lot of people conform to the societal standards of wealth and spend their hard-earned, limited funds trying to appear wealthy. A Gucci belt or a Louis Vuitton purse can only take you so far once all pictures are posted and you are back at your apartment with yourself. Just as wealth is a mindset, so is poverty. Do not back yourself into a corner and believe you are worth less than others because of materialistic belongings. Take pride in knowing that what you want will be different from others. Figure out what it means to be wealthy within you.

As mentioned, wealth is not defined to a certain demographic. A man who is in debt can claim wealth just by having the right mindset. He may be in debt, but perhaps he has a plan to get out of the debt and build himself a life. This is a wealthy mindset. Clear your thoughts of negative energy and believe that everything exists in abundance. There is enough in the world for you to become all you can be and all you want to be with the right approach. There is an abundance of money, of love, and of resources in this world. Doors will close to the ones who believe that the world is rigged towards them, and they will open once one realizes that all they need to be wealthy is, well... themselves. So step aside from the victim mindset and recognize the gaps that need to be filled in order to become wealthy. Do not limit yourself to materialistic belongings when thinking about wealth, as that is the wrong way to approach it.

Old money- the truly wealthy- seldom walk around with branded clothing worth thousands. Heck, the richest men in the world walk around in jeans, cheap sneakers, and black short-sleeves. These people have mastered what it means to be truly wealthy. They have experienced massive income and realized money comes and goes and it is up to you to change the narrative. Will your salary enter into your bank account and just stay there, or will it be invested and valued to grow and work for you?

Adjusting your mindset, lifestyle and brand is the first step to setting yourself up on the course to success. Once you are ready and determined to make the changes, the rest will follow. Removing yourself from your old environment and train of thought and adapting a new one, will open many doors and bring-in more just because you changed the way you think about things. If you make the decision to feel wealthy and be wealthy, wealth will begin and continue to make its way to you throughout the ups and the downs.

Keep in mind that throughout this book, our goal is to break the cycle of not having enough and making the best out of what you have at the moment. It is alright to want more, but recognize that having more means working more. You will likely not be able to set up generational wealth through the means of working and saving. The money you save will sit in an account and collect dust. You must invest your money; therefore, let your money collect interest and make money from existing money. This subject and how to leverage yourself best in financial situations, will be discussed in greater depth as you read along.

Anyone Can Be Wealthy

Anyone can be wealthy and that is true because wealth is a mindset. Anyone can claim wealth in their lives without millions in the bank, and do it with a proud face. As well, anyone can decide that they will be wealthy one day. People do not have to be born into money to ensure their children are born into it. The inheritance, the wealth, and the lifestyle must begin its journey somewhere. Money does not rain down from the clouds, and it sure does not grow on trees either. Money is hidden in places like a side-hustle or a promotion. You just have to work hard enough to find it.

As mentioned earlier in the text, it is important to keep in mind the type of energy we choose to let loose. Being mindful about your environment is also key. The saying 'dress for the role you want' was truly helpful, and was not said without some backing to it. Dressing for the role you want, speaking for the role you want, and making friends for the role you want are all great ways to begin changing your mindset. It is essential to also closely follow the mindset to achieve a better you and, thus, a better lifestyle. Changing your mindset is a big part of changing your old life to the new one you wish to have.

Even if you do not think you have the financial means to support the lifestyle you want, it truly is possible just by discovering what wealth means to you and becoming financially literate. By staying realistic when thinking about such things, it will become apparent pretty quickly that in order to become wealthy on your own terms, you need to learn how to manage your money a little better than what you have before. Throughout the book, you will learn how to analyze your spending and your patterns, how to invest and save, and how to spend your money while creating a spending chart that works for you.

Having the mindset that you must come from money in order to be successful is one that will hold you back. Every success story has to have started from somewhere; and just think how lucky you are if your legacy can begin with you. You may come from humble beginnings, but humble beginnings do not have to come from you.

Therefore you, an average working-class citizen, can decide on a random Tuesday morning of May that you are wealthy. Now, all you have to do is decide what being wealthy means to you, and how you will acquire said wealth.

The Aspects of Life

Although life differs from person to person, we all need money to survive. Some of us need more, some less, and some have to work for it while others can enjoy their time without worry. Different walks of life require different strategies but nonetheless, you must have a plan. If you struggle with debt, it is unfair to assume that you are bad with money inherently. A lot of people struggle with debt because they cannot afford their homes, groceries or diapers for their babies. This can be a result of independence or scarce resources- not necessarily always monetary.

Try to think about what life means to you, and what your life has been like so far. What has your main focus been? It could be family, career, money or even friends. While your career makes you money, career and money are not necessarily the same thing. If making money is your focus, then your job is just a means for you to make money. On the other hand, if your career is where your attention is mostly focused, then money is not the biggest factor in the say. People who have this mindset are usually in jobs that are paying above livable wages that allow the person to cover all necessary expenses, their wants-such as a nice vacation- and save on top of that. In this scenario, the person no longer has to worry about the lower levels of the hierarchy triangle and can focus on bigger things, such as self fulfilment that may come from being in a position of success and power.

This is not to say that any certain aspect is right or wrong. Your aspect is your aspect and should not shift or change based on a book or what anyone else has to say about it. If money is your motive, that is not to say that is better or it is more shallow than having your career at the frontier. It might, however, mean that at this point in your life your financial needs have yet to be met. Then, you might not be able to make ends meet to pay expenses such as utilities. Once again, we can consider Maslow's Hierarchy of Needs in this instance.

Maslow's Hierarchy of Needs is as follows:

- Physiological Needs
- Safety Needs

- Social Needs
- Esteem Needs
- Self-Actualization

Physiological needs are referred to as your basic needs in order to live in society as a member. These are the basic things that humans need and usually do not have to worry too much about in the Western World. It includes shelter, food, sleep, and even breathing. These things must be met before you can move on to the next stage of the triangle and it works the same all the way around. One level must be met before proceeding to the next. Someone who is homeless is likely will not be thinking about finding love, or making art or much of anything else until they are able to find a proper shelter. Once they have found this shelter, maybe then they can move on to worrying about the next level of the hierarchy.

Once your basic needs are met, we can now consider the next level of the triangle which is the safety level. This stage of the hierarchy is quite literally the feeling of being safe. Whether it be in your own home, at work or just while strolling through your day, it needs to be certain that your safety needs are met so that you are able to focus on other things. An example of these needs not being met might be in places of warlike times where there is a constant fear of occupation or attacks happening. It might also be someone who lives in a rather remote or unsafe part of town, and so they are up all night worrying or can not enjoy their home the way that they should due to the fear of their safety at play.

So now that you have your basic needs and the feeling of safety, you can now consider social needs. Your social needs are more so love and the feeling of giving and receiving love. Whether it be love from a family, friend or intimacy from your significant other, feeling of love is what makes us human and feel alive with a purpose. Although it may seem a lot less crucial than the two before it, the feeling of love gives one a purpose and may determine the aspect of your life and what is most important to you. More often than not, people will list their loved ones as their most prized and appreciated part or aspect of their lives.

Once the feeling of love from those who surround you is there and satisfied, you can now move on to esteem needs. It may seem that external needs of love come before internal feelings of love but it often is related. When you feel loved by someone else, it will be easier to love yourself as well. This esteem level not only refers to feeling of self-love but also feeling accomplished as well. This may be where people whose careers are the most important to them reside. It is the feeling of achievement, accomplishment and pride in oneself. At this stage, it might also seem that you require the respect of others more than the usual as well. Building of confidence and the feeling that you are doing something with your life.

The last and final stage of Maslow's Hierarchy of Needs is not always fulfilled, it is the level of esteem. A lot of adults never make it past the esteem level of the hierarchy, and some never even get there. Whether it may be due to the regrets of their lives, or a feeling that they are not where they are supposed to be, they do not fulfill this level. This is why it is important to realize yourself and your potential before even beginning anything else. This self-actualization level of the triangle refers to the creative, spontaneous, and artistic state of mind. Artists and people who are naturally artistically gifted might find themselves able to grasp this idea better than others. Expressing yourself and doing so without a care in the world because all other levels have been fulfilled and there is nothing more to worry about.

You may want to consider this in your financial journey to figure out where you stand and what the next stage for you might be. It is easier to keep track of your progress in this way when a precedent has already been set as a guide for you.

You have to trace back your financial struggles to your earlier life and upbringing. Are you perhaps bad with money because your parents never had enough? Or maybe they had an abundance at one point and spent carelessly until it caught up and you no longer have enough?

CHAPTER 2

Thoughts Equals Outcome

As mentioned in the earlier chapter, thoughts are a great source of bringing upon a different outlook on life, and therefore lifestyle upon yourself. Although the thought process is quite important, it is not the sole thing to make you wealthy or get you where you need to be. You can sit and think about becoming a millionaire all you desire, but without the proper actions, you will likely not achieve this daydream. When I speak on thoughts within this book, I do not mean an empty passing thought. When I mention a thought, I am referring to an active process of coming up with a plan and strategy to achieve your goals and then manifesting them to life.

A great example of this can be related to job hunts. One cannot sit in a spot for hours and think of being employed and expect the opportunity to spring up and land on your lap. However, if you think about being employed, then think about ways to pursue employment then you can expect a positive outcome. Your thought process should be:

- Put together a resume that accurately captures your past employment and experience, then tailor it to the field you want to pursue. For example, if you want to go into accounting, do not include your babysitting job.

- When your resume has been drafted, have someone with greater experience in the field, or a trusted friend with a proper understanding of grammar edit it for you. It would be most beneficial to have your resume circulate between various people to get the best feedback. Fix your resume accordingly.

- Once you are satisfied with your resume, begin searching for jobs in the area you would like to work in. For example, if you desire an accounting job in New York but are currently in a state halfway across the country, hit the internet and look for firms in the Washington area. Be sure to proactively look for firms that match what you want out of the job such as pay, benefits and work-life balance.

- At this time, you can begin manifesting finding a job that fits your description of the best employment.

- Once you have determined several firms that are suitable for your employment, begin drafting cover letters catered to the specific firm and role you are applying for. Be sure not to come off too desperate but not to aloof either.

- With your custom cover letter and edited resume, you can now begin sending in your applications. You can do this by way of job boards, or emailing them directly to their Human Resources department.

- This step is once again a place to manifest and let your thoughts bring forth positive energy because you have done the work. When all there is left to do but wait to hear back from these firms, begin thinking about how happy you will be at the given job.

This process can be applied to any given situation you put yourself in. If your goal is not to find employment, but to invest in properties, you should approach it the same way. Begin by stating clearly what you want. "I want to own a home to rent out by the end of the year." You have established a clear goal. Now, do some internal research and consider whether you have saved up money for a down payment, your disposable income, how much you can spare to save for this occasion, bank loans and the area you wish to purchase the home in. Then, go ahead and begin your external research into the home market, and once you have a clear understanding, begin looking for a real estate agent. Although it is not necessary to do business with an agent, it may be the best way to see some homes in person you would not have otherwise been aware of. Once you have picked a home that fits your wants and needs, employ a home inspector. If the home inspector deems the house healthy, begin negotiations with the owners. Be sure your real estate agent is honest and wants the best for you and not just out for the commission. Then purchase your home and begin looking for tenants. You can do this by listing the property on a social site such as Facebook Marketplace and ask applicants to send in a piece of ID, bank statements and letter of reference. Find the best suitor by analyzing credit scores, criminal history, disposable income, and finally by meeting them in person. Once you draft up a lease agreement, you have provided an outcome from a passive thought.

At this stage, it is important to stress the difference between a passive thought and an active thought. A thought is passive and will not bear any fruit until a plan of action and a strategy is thought of as well, making it an active thought. And so, the most important takeaway from this chapter is to spend time thinking but not just that. The idea is to extend your thoughts to contingencies, to different possibilities, and to the opportunities that will come your way.

Passive thoughts can be allowed and are inevitable, but should be followed by active thoughts. Every thought you have that comes in passing must be followed by a thought of action. Even if your passive thought is that your car is running low on fuel, your next thought should be to think about nearby gas stations, gas prices, and time management considering when to get fuel and still make it to work on time. Passive thoughts come and go, but they are meaningless without actions. It is helpful to allow them to come, but do not let them pass without a game plan. Keeping this in mind in all aspects of life will allow for you to have more meaningful experiences, and plan for everything without even noticing it. Practicing active thinking over time will pour out into everything you do and before you know it, you will not be able to have a thought without thinking twice.

Positive Manifestation

As mentioned, manifestation is quite powerful but not very outcome-bearing on its own. So then, what exactly is manifestation? Manifesting something is the practice of bringing opportunity and desires to you. It is a little more intensive than a simple thought and requires a little more work.

To manifest positive happenings into your life, begin by clearing your thoughts of things that are holding you back. Referring back to the employment scenario, do not block your blessings by putting negative energy into the universe by putting yourself down or doubting yourself. You would not tell your child or best friend that they cannot do something or that they do not stand a chance- so why speak to yourself in such a manner?

Here are two positive manifestation techniques to help you along:

- Manifesting in the Mind: Imagine yourself where you wish to be. Retired, with x amount of money in the bank. Savings maxed out and the mortgage paid off. What does the ideal life look like to you? Do not give in to temptations and imagine a life that is too far off. Do not trade your wife for Megan Fox and do not imagine that you become a billionaire by tomorrow. Stick to your very realistic goals and what you are actually WORKING towards right now. Try to stick to short-term goals like imagining yourself working at the same firm you applied to last week. What does that look like to you? What does the office space feel like? Try to soak in all feelings from your mind and manifestation. The feeling you get is important for this exercise. Think about what you wear, what you would say, and how you would fit in. You can do the same when thinking about reaching a certain number in your savings or paying off school debts. Anything that you are actively working towards, you can begin to manifest.

- Journal Manifestation: Go shopping and buy a journal with the purpose of manifesting it. It can be a dollar store cheap one, but it must be purchased for its purpose rather than one that has been laid around your house without one. In this journal, you will write down your manifestations. You will repeat these three times a day for various amounts. You will write down your manifestation three times in the morning after slumber, six times in the afternoon and nine more times before heading to bed. This method, employed by many who believe in manifesting, has been called the key to the universe by important figures like Nikola Tesla.

Not only do these methods bring forth your manifestations, but also do a good job of reminding you of the goals at-hand. Writing something down 18 times a day, or thinking about it vividly with no interruptions for five minutes a day will greatly affect your lifestyle and shape it to fit your goals.

Winner Mindset

Mentioned at least a billion times, both in this book and in life, the power of thought is real and true. Let's do an experiment. Go stand in front of the mirror and look at yourself. I bet after a couple of seconds you begin noticing flaws about yourself. Uneven jawline, crooked nose, shifted teeth from not wearing your retainers. Probably even more if you kept looking. Now, you have thought about your flaws and have it in your head that you are not all that and a bag of chips.

The winner mindset should be a part of who you are at this point. If you say something enough times, you will begin to believe it. Affirmations might help in this case. Here are some daily affirmations that you should repeat to yourself in the mirror after waking up from sleep in the morning:

- "I am a winner. Everything I do, I do well and I am the best at what I do. No one could be a better fit than me at what I do."

- "I do not chase, I attract. What is meant for me, will always find me in the end."

- "Money is not a problem to me. Money flows through me. I attract money and money finds me."

- "There is no one better than me to live my life. I was made for the life that I live and I am grateful to be the one."

- "I am enough to be successful. I will become the best version of me."

- "I have overcome all challenges, I will overcome all challenges. Nothing wears or tears me down. I am made for the hard stuff."

- "What others think of me is not my business. I am a winner and winners worry about their own success."

- "I am beauty, I am charming, I am charismatic and I am me in all shapes and forms."

- "I am the best me and no one could be me better than me. I do not want to become someone else because I am the powerhouse that I need."

- "I have not reached my potential. I am powerful and I am strong and I will do everything to reach my goals."

These are 10 of the most powerful affirmations that may give you a better idea on where to begin with a winner mindset. Simply stand in front of your mirror in the morning and try to repeat these affirmations to yourself about five times. Say it with confidence and say it while looking into your eyes. These affirmations should come from a place of confidence and you should believe it yourself as you are saying them. You are not trying to convince yourself of these statements at this point, but only reminding yourself. Remember that you have made it this far and you can make it more.

Go take a break and listen to some of your favorite hype tracks from your gym playlist with a confident stroke to it. Let yourself loose and dance around a little. Let the lyrics get to your head. Yeah! You are the baddest one in the room! At the peak of your hype, go look in the same mirror. I bet those flaws are looking a lot less relevant now and the focus is more so on your badass dancing skills. I bet you feel a lot more confident too, and we can tell in your talk, your walk, and the way you carry yourself- and it looks much better than the first one did. This is the power of thought. The mental state you put yourself in is just that. You are a victim of your own insecurities and negative thought process.

Another thing to draw attention to on this topic is breaking out of the norm. We have and will talk more greatly about you being a product of your environment and being the average of the handful of people you are the closest to. This is very true, and another aspect is to break out of that social norm that seems to hold so many people back. There are many things that may seem like they are alright just because they are highly accepted in society. The question to ask here is, is it okay for you? Are the standards that are held on a pedestal by others the same for your purposes? Consider these questions greatly moving forward.

This could also correlate with the people you hang around as well. If all of your friends are in debt while you are debt-free, you might be the best out of all of them and feel you are in the best place because you are above the average of what you know. But then consider if that is something to really hold to a high standard. You are debt free, but do you have enough money left for a savings account, investment account and your retirement fund? Now, remove yourself from your normal environment and the people you usually hang around and imagine you are now placed in a room full of five other people you hold to a high standard, but keep it realistic. This may be your father in law, or your own father and their friends, whoever it may be. Now, you being the same person that you are and having the same fiscal responsibilities and the same salary, how would you land in that room?

You should never compare yourself to others who are below you just to make yourself feel a little better. Instead, understand that you need motivation and not fluffing. Compare yourself to those who you consider to be in a better position than you whether it be financially or professionally. If you fall short, brainstorm ways that you can catch up to them and match their standards instead. If you are just about at the match of them, then consider picking other people or mentors to look up to and connect with. You should always be looking for ways to better yourself and never holding yourself back. There are always goals to reach and gaps to fill. Bettering yourself is not a process that stops at any one point. Understand that it is forever continuous.

What is holding you back at the moment? Are you afraid to explore a different field in your career or too scared to make any purchases in the stock market? "Scared money don't make no money", a wise man once said. Do your research and make informed decisions, but do not let your fears and doubts get in the way of you reaching your full potential.

CHAPTER 3

Values Alignment

One thing that is often discussed and debated in finances is where values lie. Where does the value of your bank lie? What about that one CEO everyone is talking about right now? And, the richest man in the world? It seems that as time goes on and people become more empathetic and able to have a platform, these questions are addressed more and more. However, values do not often mix with finances in the real world. Just think, your favorite fast-fashion site employs children and your favorite bank invests other people's money.

Keep remembering, you are not an institution. You are an individual who must stay in one body and mind forever. So, you must find it within yourself to ask the question of where your values lie.

What are values? Values are things or actions you hold to a high degree, revolving around ethics. Your values are what you determine as the best possible thing one can do in any given situation. Now, values sound superior, but they are not always positive, nor do they have to be. Values may also contradict each other at times and maybe for the sole purpose of benefit and gain. For example, a company's values may rest on making the best possible decision for the organization and its shareholders. And though that sounds promising enough, the best possible decision for the organization and its shareholders is to increase profits wherever they can. This may mean taking shortcuts, employing in other countries for cheaper and worse conditions, or employing methods that harm the environment.

So, you see, values can always sound honorable and as if it is the right thing to do, but some consider a closer look. Our purpose is not to deceive others or bring upon harm, but to a better life for ourselves and those who come after us. The purpose of this chapter is to bring light to the reason for your financial awakening. You have at one point realized that you are not satisfied with your capital achievements and have decided to turn it around. Likely, you have read many articles concerning making money and surely you have Googled: "How to get rich quick" more than once. This is not reality. The image of becoming a success overnight are fairy tale stories people feed you to buy their product, or even worse buy into their superior image. Nothing gets done without some elbow grease.

You must do the same for yourself, but also consider other factors-more than the companies care for anyway. Re-evaluate the things that are the most important to you and begin making decisions based on what you come up with. If your values are family, maybe you want to invest in real estate so that you can leave behind a home for your family? Or you may want to look into life insurance to take the burden off your family in your greater absence?

At the end of the day, your values are what makes you the person that you are. Your values are what dictates your life, and you should be careful to not stray far from your values for disposable and temporary things such as money. While financial income is quite important when building a life, values hold a similar weight when doing so. For this chapter, a good exercise to try revolving around values, is to write what each value is for you and what it means to you. Then, write down an instance in your life for each where you have sacrificed that value for something else, and another instance in life where you had the opportunity to disregard your values but stuck to them. Now compare your answers for both and spot the differences. Why was one scenario fair play to disregard your values while the other one was not enough to do so? Once you have arrived at your answer, discuss with yourself if another scenario should arrive that would require you to overlook your values, would you take it? What would it depend on?

Now, consider your values at the present tense and your lifestyle right now. Then, consider your ideal lifestyle and way of life. Consider which values would match the lifestyle you have in mind and which ones would not make the cut. Nothing you do right now should be for the moment. Every aspect of your life, including your values should revolve around the fact that you are on a road to becoming a better you. Every thought you have should be wired to ensure that the ideal you would benefit from having these thoughts, or in this case, having these values. Changing your values is quite hard and may not be possible, but it is hoped that your values would not have to change in order to lead a better lifestyle.

A cheat code to this may be to remember your role models and people you look up to in this sense. You can pick a variety of people who impress you from people you look up to financially, to people who do advocacy work all around the world. Now, do some research and figure out what these people value in their lives. It might be a good idea to jot them down at this time. You might be seeing a pattern or repetition of some values, or an appearance by values that you never gave much time to. Analyze them all and decide for yourself which of these values you think you should be focused on as well. When doing this, it might be good to ask yourself if the value you have picked to reflect on yourself is one that has helped this person attain a position of success or if this value might not have had much to do with it. People with varying amounts of passion and values are able to become their ideal selves all of the time. Then, decide on the person you want to be.

You might find this part of the text to be the hardest part to get around. That is alright. Below, we have compiled some exercises and further explanations for you to get a better grasp on what we are trying to display. At the end of the day, it is you who must live with your values and make decisions based on them. Be sure to not stray too far away from yourself.

Discover Your Values

We will begin by trying an exercise. Grab a piece of paper and a pen. Sit down where you will not be disturbed for the remainder of this exercise, and try to clear your head of intrusive thoughts. Then, think of the three most important things in life to you at this moment. Are these temporary things, or things that will change in a 5-year period? If the answer is yes, begin the exercise over until your answer to those questions is a firm 'no'. Once you have established the three most important things in life to you that are permanent and will likely not change over the course of five years, you have identified your values in life. The next thing to figure out is how to improve, adjust or change your life in order to fulfill these values. Keep in mind that when determining such things, it is alright and advised to remain a little selfish. Do not only think about those that come after you, or people dearest to you but throw yourself into the mix as well. This is your life, and you should be valued by yourself the most.

My Values:

1.

2.

3.

Are they permanent?   Yes   No

Will they change in five years? Likely   Not Likely

Once you have filled it out, keep these values in mind at all times. Remember why they are values and the purpose of this exercise (to adjust your lifestyle to fit these values). If your lifestyle already supports your values, you are lucky and should focus on greater values to establish. There must be more than three things in the world that are important to you.

Another exercise that might help you understand the type of person that you are might be through making use of a personality test. Use this link here: https://www.16personalities.com/free-personality-test to take the test. Answer all questions truthfully, and as accurately as possible. At the end, carefully read up on your result. It will be one of the 16 personality types. Read up on yours and see if it matches up with who you are. If you are not sure, do further research. If you still do not feel it represents you accurately, consider taking the test again and giving your answers a bit more thought.

Grounding

Grounding is a way that we can feel more human and more at peace with the state we are in at the moment. Grounding can take on many forms and should be special to the person and the type of situation involved. People often turn to grounding exercises after a tough time at work or a particularly stressful time in their lives.

To emphasize the importance of decision making, it might be in your best interest to take the time to try some of these grounding exercises to make sure that your decisions are not being made solely out of emotion. Grounding yourself, calming down and finding reason in what you are doing will make your future-self thank you.

Although there are many ways to ground yourself and discover your intentions, here are a couple of preferred ways to practice:

- Pick a sunny day after a rainy one and find a smooth field of grass to walk on. At this moment, remove your shoes and socks and other restriction items such as a backpack or tight jewelry. Walk around the field for a couple of moments, taking heavy steps and minding the cool mud and moist grass on the sole of your feet. Allow your mind to wander to all different places before focusing on the issue that is at hand. Now, take some time to ponder on your values and what they might sound like to say out loud.

- After a day of dealing with your daily tasks, grab a journal or piece of paper and sit where you will be disturbed for several minutes or however long you need. Now, take yourself back to your upbringing and pick and choose 'bad' and 'good' things your parents did financially or otherwise. Now, pick from that list what you would like to bring moving forward with your financial journey and which ones are better left in the past. If you have a partner whose finances are concerned with your own, this exercise should be done together and results should be a topic of discussion.

- Pick an object in the room you are currently in and focus on it. Make sure it is an inanimate object that does not move. Shut all outside noises down and be at the moment with that particular object. Notice every little imperfection and characteristics on its surface. Really examine the thing. Then, slowly begin focusing on your breathing. Now bring the attention to your feet and make sure they are planted on the floor with your heels. If you need to or can, stand up at this time to get a better feeling. Take your time and do not acknowledge anything external until you are ready to do so.

You might find that these exercises might be best practiced alone. We suggest you take some time in a quiet area to perform these exercises. If you are on this journey with a partner, try meditating together but not grounding. Breathing exercises and some journaling could also be done in a coupled environment.

It might help you to begin journaling your grounding exercises as well. You may notice a pattern between certain times when you need grounding. These may be times of particularly high stress such as University finals or quarterly employee check-in at work. If you can track down a pattern, you might now be able to better understand why these things require grounding. If possible, you might be able to avoid these things or brainstorm more effective exercises to try to prevent the buildup of so much stress, rather than waiting until the moment it happens to deal with it.

CHAPTER 4

What About the Money

It seems that I have rambled on about a lot of stuff that does not include dolla dolla bills...what about the money? Getting rich or becoming financially literate cannot be expected to be conquered overnight. It is a process of learning, and takes some prerequisite knowledge and understanding in order for it to truly stick with you. Likewise, first, I want to focus on learning the basics of wealth, understanding your own values and how those relate to your financial journey and the power of thought are all essential knowledge as we move forward with our lessons.

It seems that people who do not have the money seem to think they would know exactly what to do with it, while people in possession of capital may seem to be spending it in the wrong places. The truth is, there is no right or wrong way to spend your own hard-earned money. However, there is a wrong way to execute your spending plan by dabbling in purchases and expenses that are out of your means. As your income increases and investments pay off, so will your expenses. With a promotion comes a larger salary and maybe the need to upgrade other parts of your lifestyle as well. Bigger house with a bigger mortgage, a new car with a sizable car note and so on. While these things may seem to be within your means at the moment and necessary to match the lifestyle you had in mind (not to mention the thrill of fitting in with people who used to be above your tax bracket), every decision you make should involve long-term plans. Keep in mind that temporary is the present, but forever is the future.

Your money is a resource for you to get where you need to go in life- treat it as such. And while money may come and go without any way to take it with you to the grave, money is still the answer to many things in life. Our purpose is to break generational curses of living from paycheck to paycheck and to ensure the generation after us does not have to struggle as we did. As simple enough as it sounds, getting there is quite the journey. Knowing money and what it can do for you and the lifestyle you want and the legacy you leave behind is the ultimate goal.

While working is one of the main ways most people acquire their income, it is not the only way to do so. Money can come from jobs, sure, but investing is also another great way to make some money as well. I will touch on this subject in later chapters, but the most important thing when beginning to invest is to do a full research on everything. Research everything from the origin of the stock market to historical trends and changes, such as the 2008 housing bubble. Everything is truly connected with one another when it comes to investment. A popular trend these days is bitcoin and although it may be quite risky, it can be a great payoff in huge amounts. It might also pay off to follow up on the activities of Tesla's owner, Elon Musk, since everything he touches seems to be gold in the stock market.

With this said, the money for investing has to come from somewhere. Discovering your passions and turning them into paid gigs and side hustles can be another way of earning some extra income. Finding a way to make money from social media such as TikTok accounts for your baking adventures on the weekends may make you some money on the side if you know how to operate. Gaining a following and posting quality content that people want to see will likely get you invited to the creator fund, and you can eventually make some good money by doing what you love. The same scenarios can also happen on other sites, such as YouTube, where a channel could be started where you vlog your day, or your shopping spree tour of the week. An Instagram page dedicated to your puppy is another idea, and so on and so forth. People make all sorts of cash posting about all sorts of things online. If this is not so much your wave, consider other small things that might make you some extra cash on the side such as walking dogs couple times a week when you would already be taking your own dogs on walks anyways. These side hustles should be a way to make some extra money as an addition to your regular job. The side hustle(s) should also be focused mainly on your passions and hobbies rather than the money. You are already working for the money, so your side hustle should be about something more and something that you can actually enjoy doing.

Remember that money is a product of your hard work, but can also come and go. It is definitely easier coming than going, but it must be understood that money is meant to be spent and necessities require monetary exchanges. On the contrasting end, while money is meant to be spent, it should also be valued as it fulfills many needs for us and is a product of hard work. Saving it, investing it and letting it grow is essentially what we are aiming for.

Lifestyle Wants Vs What You Have

The lifestyle you have is what you have been conditioned to accept. You may even be proud of where you are today when comparing yourself to others or your own upbringing. This is a common mistake because although you can absolutely be happy and proud of yourself, you should never accept that where you are right now is the best it gets. A better life is just one good habit away.

Knowing this, you need to recognize your regular routine and pick out habits that you have been doing. Analyze spending patterns by reviewing your bank statements, pay attention to how often you use cash and how much regularly is put into your investment and/or savings accounts. When you can identify and point out unnecessary spending habits such as buying $10 worth of coffee daily when you have a perfectly capable, and frankly expensive coffee machine at home, we can cut this problem at its root. Although breaking a habit is easily one of the hardest things to do in life, the first step is to acknowledge that change must be brought. Once you realize that something needs to change in order for you to reach your goals, you will be more inclined to do so.

Circling back to the coffee example; the act of buying coffee is not simply the coffee you buy. There are a lot of hidden costs and opportunity costs that are also thrown out the window. When you buy the coffee, you likely want something to quickly eat, sometimes to go with your drink, and so by adding another five dollars to your order, bringing the price up to $15. This is likely a daily occurrence, assuming that you only buy coffee on weekdays on the way to work. The math in this scenario looks like this:

- $15 (daily order total) x 5 (days placing the order) = $75 a week x 4 (weeks) = $300 a month

- In this situation, assume the investment account you have placed it into has around a 3.75% return on investment

- Now, you can see that you do not simply spend $10 or even $15 but $311.25 in a single month. (You just made the price of your daily coffee just buy letting your money work for you) Now compare this price to some of your monthly bills; probably could pay off two or three of your bills.

- As well, you have to wake up early each morning to leave the house early to make it to work on time after your trip to the coffee shop. Perhaps you can leave about 20 minutes earlier daily. These are 2o precious minutes that you could have used towards a more productive lifestyle, such as reading or stretching in the morning.

When you begin to realize your harmful habits and unnecessary spending with a fully backed logic, you begin to associate the difference between spoiling yourself with a coffee now and spoiling yourself with a car in two years. Changing your lifestyle has to begin with your mindset. You must first understand that you cannot dream of a different and better lifestyle when you make no plans to better your current self and situation.

Your old habits and lifestyle will simply keep you in the same spot. Expecting different results from the same actions is madness, and change must first begin within you. Recognize your bad habits, and make a physical list if you must. Review your bank account weekly to highlight any spending getting in the way of you and your ideal lifestyle. Have others with better habits and people who already have the lifestyle you are working for critique your lifestyle or even observe them in order to see if there are certain gaps in your life you can fill.

Habits Accordingly

Habits are perhaps the most crucial component of changing your lifestyle. Habits are what define you, from the most mundane of tasks to the ones you put effort into. There are full blown careers that are focused on just the science of building and eliminating habits. Most of the marketing sector and many of the successful companies we have known to love today have done so because of their ability to create a habit. Pay attention to your habits and see if there is a lesson to be learned or something that needs to be fixed. There are several ways to go about such changes.

Did you know people did not regularly brush their teeth not that long ago? Only reason why brushing your teeth is essential several times a day is because of some great marketing people that understood the need to create a habit among the people. The old toothpaste people used to brush their teeth had no taste, smell or tingly feeling to it. And right now, the minty fresh feeling of toothpaste has not proven to be better at cleaning teeth or fighting off bacteria. Toothpaste has evolved into smelling and tasting the way it does to be distinguished a certain way and alert people when it is time to brush their teeth. It is now universally accepted that we must brush our teeth when we wake up and before slumber, and sometimes even in between. And the feeling that we are looking for is the tingly, fresh feeling of mint in our mouths to wash away the taste of whatever is in our mouths. This is a habit that marketers have created long ago, but has changed the dynamic of the world as we know it. Brushing teeth might seem small but is a multibillion-dollar industry thanks to understanding the science of habit making.

First, you must recognize the bad habits. For example, a lazy habit of lounging in bed for hours on our phone before deciding to start our day; this is not productive or beneficial in any way and a habit that needs to be reformed. Now the next step is to decide on a habit that will take the place of the old one. In this case, we decide that when we wake up, we will immediately get up out of our beds and begin morning stretches. We can decide to put on YouTube videos in the beginning, and then move towards freestyling once a new routine is established. Now, perhaps the hardest part is applying the behavior. You need to do this by implementing it immediately. Do not wait for a new week to start, do not wait five minutes after waking up to begin your routine. Whatever you decided on in the planning process is what you need to stick to.

Habits that are unproductive and not useful often have a tendency to have negative effects anyway. For example, the hours you have wasted on your phone, whatever it may be, could have been the time spent bettering yourself or making money or researching ways to invest money. It is important to keep in mind the opportunity costs of our actions and not just accept them at face value.

It is also important to note that habits differ from the time you allot to enjoy yourself and your life. Just because you are making the decision to limit or eliminate unnecessary phone time in the mornings does not mean you should never be allowed to aimlessly scroll on TikTok. Understanding and delegating times to be disciplined and other times to be free and enjoy your time make all the difference. For example, although your day should not start in such an unproductive manner, there is absolutely no harm in performing the same activity at nighttime before bed when all tasks are finished and you feel accomplished for the day.

CHAPTER 5

Emotional Charge

The emotional factor is often an overlooked factor when considering finances and might be considered not as important, but that is far from the truth. Our emotions cause us to perform acts that may be harmful or beneficial in our journey to becoming financially responsible and stable. Our emotions guide many of our actions.

Consider a very emotionally charged day, whether it may be a breakup or an embarrassing day at work, these are negative-emotion-charged days. You are prone to more careless behavior and spending more out of emotion to soothe yourself. You may find on these days, the urge to spend is higher and the things you are spending on are unnecessary and temporary. These orders include takeout food, therapy shopping for clothes or paying to rent movies you have already seen. And although it is extremely important to take care of yourself and make yourself feel better after a long and hard day, the focus should shift from temporary fixes to things that keep you occupied while building your personal empire.

Instead of turning to comfort food, consider cleaning your room for a boost of serotonin. Instead of shopping for new clothes, try on the ones you have and begin listing the ones on sites like Depop of Poshmark for some extra side cash from clothing you no longer wear. Instead of renting Footloose to watch it for the 100th time, consider watching a financially educated or inspiring movie such as The Big Short. There are many resources to deal with emotionally hard days. It is up to you to decide how you take control and deal with them.

Being emotionally charged is most certainly a negative thing and something that is not desirable in a person, especially a person who is looking to make some changes to their finances. Work on your inner emotions and operate on something other than emotions and feelings at the moment. As most of us know, the best motivators are negative energy and so if you are someone who is easily emotionally manipulated, try using the high levels of negative energy as a means to help you. If you feel angry, sad, confused or mad then consider turning those emotions into actions that will benefit your life in the long run. Go for a run, a jog, cook or do some reading in the quiet by yourself.

Getting carried away with being emotionally charged is not something one can afford to get away with when attempting to change their life around. Shifting your mindset from its ancient way of thinking is obviously challenging and may require some work but it certainly is not impossible. While solutions such as therapy or other sessions and workshops may require a lot of time, money and other resources, the activities and exercises covered in this book are a lot more suitable. Meditating, finding yourself and becoming one with the lifestyle you wish to have are all signs of working to improve yourself and may help in the process of emotionally detaching yourself from making decisions that may not be the best for yourself or your goals.

Although being emotional is often depicted as a negative thing in today's world, we must do our best to beat out the stigma. Being emotional might lead you to make some decisions that you would not have otherwise been up for. Emotional changes to your life can come from a place of happiness and positivity as well. A decision to purchase stock to support a friend who has begun their first day of work there is a nice gesture of support that can go a long way. As well, a decision made based on a negative event or occurrence can create positive outcomes. For example, the decision to become financially stable might come from a place of sorrow and hardship, but you will certainly find yourself coming out of the other end of the tunnel as a better person.

Good can come from emotional people and decisions, sure but it also must be kept in check. Emotional big decisions should be limited and especially when it comes to your finances. This is because your financial matters should always be monitored and any changes or decisions should be based on knowledge and research. It may be hard to differentiate between the two when emotions are involved. And so, while it is great to show emotions every chance and in any form, they may come in the real world, it is important to be able to establish boundaries as well.

When dealing with being emotionally charged, it is important to respect your own boundaries as well. Recognizing when your emotions are getting the best of you and taking the time to reflect and return is important. Try to stray away from any decision making or even conversations when you are in this state as you are quite vulnerable and probably insensitive to others emotions at the same time too. Step away and distance yourself from people and decision making and let yourself feel all the emotions that are running through you first. Then, when you are calmed down you can assess the situation and decide which way you would like to proceed with.

There may be many reasons for you being emotional and it is alright to let it run down as long as you are removed from any major life changing decisions. Especially stay away from investing or spending at this time. Buying or selling out of pure emotion rather than waiting on research and a sound mind will likely cause some headaches in the future. When it comes to your finances, lead with your mind not your heart. You should buy stocks or cryptocurrency from rumour and sell based on fact. Emotions are not involved in this process. If everyone acted on emotion, there would be no room for critical thinking. So the next time you catch yourself being a little too aggressive, catch a breath and wait a while before you take the next step.

While therapy is an expensive and a resource-draining option, it might be best to enroll at this time if you find yourself struggling with emotional charge. It might help you in ways you did not think prior. If you cannot afford to partake in therapy at this time, consider someone who you can trust to be your sounding board. Someone who can listen without judgement or much else to say and lets you talk things out yourself. When we seek closure, we do not always need help or guidance. Sometimes we just need someone to listen to and let us talk things out ourselves and find our own answers. Especially with making decisions, no one could possibly know what the best decision to make, other than you. You are the one who knows all details of your life and considerations and could make the best decision for yourself. While it is wise to speak to others who have had similar experiences, someone else should never be your deciding factor.

When it comes to making a decision, the end goal must always remain in the line of sight. Every decision you make in your life is a domino effect that falls down onto the next one. Keep this in mind when making the next big decision and watch how much more careful you are and how much more thought you require to reach a decision. The you that you wish to become is always just one decision away. A controlled environment is always more tame than the latter and that is easier to maintain when emotions are kept in check.

Dealing with Uncontrolled Behavior

For the days that it seems you cannot control your own behavior and are struggling to keep yourself in line, consider spending some time with a trusted friend. A friend who will call you out and direct you to a better path of dealing with emotions. This friend, as discussed earlier, should be a friend of yours with a similar mindset as you or someone who is already in the position you wish to be in. You should aim to surround yourself with individuals who are reaching goals you find impressive and/or hope to hit. You truly are who you hang around and birds of a feather do indeed flock together. Take five of your closest friends and associates, ask them for their salaries and add those numbers up and divide them by five to get the average and I bet that number is pretty darn close to what you are making.

When days come that you notice your behavior is out of hand, rely on someone else for help. While they can come and help at the moment, it is also important to remember they will not always be there for you at the time of need. Consider also other ways to keep yourself accountable. In the journal you should be keeping daily to log the occurrences of your day, be sure to include all negative aspects of your day and actions that you wish you would have done differently, could improve and regret. When writing it, you will probably open a door that will allow for more emotions and thoughts to pour out. This is good and you should be recording everything as you go. As time goes by and you think you have made some improvement, your journaling will be less heavy until you are able to talk your own self out of undesired and out of control behaviors.

An effective but expensive way to invest in yourself for uncontrolled behavior might be to seek the help of a licensed professional. It is not always to be fully in control of yourself or to rely and open up to another person, no matter how close of a friend they may be. Actively bettering yourself means putting in the effort and this is one of the many ways you can do so. Opening up, learning and keeping track of your progress and improvements can help you to become more wary of yourself in the future.

Journaling is a great way to keep in touch with yourself and in cases such as this where it is used as a tool for holding yourself accountable, it will be great to watch yourself grow and evolve. Then, read what you wrote in that book from before and reminisce and celebrate the person you have become now. You are always stronger than you were the day before. You have seen more, heard more and done more than you ever did a minute ago.

Splurging Within Your Means

In this chapter, we talked a lot about surrounding yourself with people who inspire you and push you to be better and the pitfalls of emotional spending. Through these thoughts, it was expressed how important it is to keep yourself healthy and happy while also reaching your goals. It is okay to splurge within your means- what does that mean? As the title suggests, splurging within your means is allowing yourself the room to be spoiled and loved while also being mindful of where and how your finances are affected.

This is one of my personal favorite things to touch on since it discusses the importance of spoiling and taking care of yourself while also starting within your means. This is a specialty of mine and something that I think everyone should be working on. A lot of trends and internet sharing has brainwashed some people into thinking name brands and designers are what you need to be spoiling yourself and that could not be farther from the truth. Spoiling oneself is dependent on the person and can range extremely from person to person. A vacation, a spa day, a fancy restaurant takeout meal, and yoga classes are all examples of what spoiling oneself might mean to someone. Not all of them are flashy or social media and none of them will drain your bank account.

Spoiling yourself within your means is also a great way to test your boundaries and discipline as well. Being able to downgrade your expenses and items can allow you to explore how much you are willing to sacrifice and push yourself. Making sacrifices is a big part of reaching financial stability. Living the way you are living now but expecting different outcomes is just not very realistic. You need to be able to show that you are willing to make changes and really dedicate yourself to the cause. This should be something that you want to do because you are at the end of the day, working for yourself.

While spoiling yourself is very much necessary and welcomed, you must remember that spoiling yourself doubled in the future definitely trumps spoiling yourself once over right now. Living a good life now so that you can live a great one later is one of the mottos of this book. Your career and your income at the moment will decide much of what spoiling yourself will look like. As a waitress, you might be on your feet all day and making some extra money on the weekends. To spoil yourself, you might consider picking up some extra shifts on the weekends to buy yourself an electric foot massager to take the load off after work. The foot massager has been paid for with the extra shifts you have picked up and now, you can relax while reading your favorite book on the couch. Another more immediate example of suffering for now to live for later.

If you are making $30,000 on salary with a mortgage, car payment and credit debt, and you decide you deserve a $5,500 Christian Dior bag while your insurance has not been paid… we have some reflecting to do. Consider your income, then your expenses and debt. How much can you spare to feel better about yourself? If the intention of spoiling oneself is to feel better in a given situation, I highly doubt adding on to your financial burdens will provide you with a better feeling than before. Stick to things that you can afford to spoil yourself with. Order some cute clothes on sale or order in some Chinese takeout. Make smart choices and always consider the context when deciding.

CHAPTER 6

An Intentional Life

Setting intentions seems to be a passing trend these days with everyone speaking on the importance of speaking things into the universe and manifesting. Well, there is always a reason for trends. This one, in particular, is to set an intention for your financial wealth. Where do you stand right now? Where do you wish you were? Where will you be in five years from now? 10 years? It is important to cover your bases when making decisions like finances that in turn affect many other aspects of your life.

An intentional life is a life that comes with purpose. A life where you live for the now with the knowledge of where you are headed and where you wish to be. Setting your intentions and living with intentions is quite similar to setting goals for yourself. While not exactly the same, setting intentions can refer to the life you live now and the way you wish to live it. Usually meant to be more spiritual than literal, find your passion when setting intentions. Consider a life without stress, or a life without financial burden. Would this be your intention moving forward?

To live an intentional life is to live a life with purpose. Living life everyday with no desire to better yourself or those around you, or even the world as a whole is a life and opportunity wasted. Making a conscious effort to carry out the positive intentions you set for yourself is quite possibly the most important part of your evolution to a better you. While these intentions are set for you, you should also consider the effects it has on other people and make an effort to be someone who makes positive changes to those around them.

An example of an intentional task can be to keep a cleaner space around you. This intention can be carried out in so many different ways that can benefit so many different people. Cleaning your home every other day with a deep cleanse every Saturday. Picking up garbage you see in passing and setting out with a garbage bag to intentionally clean up the streets around your neighborhood or work once a week. Making changes to clean up the office space you work at are all examples of setting an intention and then living up to it, and thus, living an intentional life.

Another way to live a more intentional life is to be aware of the experiences that you open yourself up to. Being more selective with the way you choose to spend your precious time, money and resources is a way to settle yourself into the role you want and not the role you have. Following in others footprints will play no role in making yourself any more significant. Once you establish the life you wish to have, abandon all other things you once did and set on the course that pursues what you wish to become.

Your intentions should always be set on becoming a better and more enlightened version of yourself, leaving everything you did before as a part of the old you. Sure, it is alright to keep some bits and pieces and allow yourself to have fun but it is also more important to identify things that do not add value to who you are and who you will be. So, the next time your friends invite you to do something that you are not sure of, or something that will financially set you back from achieving your goal, consider pulling back and opting out.

This is not to say that you should completely change the way you think and forget about all you have. Being grateful is another way to live an intentional life. Realizing your lifestyle is a privileged one even if it may not feel like it at times and becoming better because of it is a wonderful thing. While you may not agree to go to brunch with your friends every week to do better for yourself, acknowledging that you are privileged enough to even be offered it is enough.

Meditating regularly is also another way to keep yourself grounded and make sure that you are sticking true to yourself and your goals. Meditation is known to help people focus and concentrate not only in the moment, but throughout their daily tasks as well. Especially people with conditions such as ADHD, OCD and even anger management. These conditions that affect your daily life by making it more difficult to be present in the moment and see things for how they are rather than your version. Meditation aims to blur out the irrelevant bits by helping your brain focus on the more important things such as the way you are feeling and what your next moves will be moving forward.

Living an intentional life is hard to get right but once you do, you will feel the best you have ever felt. Knowing that you are finally on the path that you were supposed to be will be worth every missed event. Once again, do not limit yourself to the point that you are no longer enjoying yourself and are only looking forward to the future. Living an intentional life just means you know what path to be on, not fully disregarding everything else that makes life fun. Enjoying the now while not getting caught up is the key to living an intentional life.

Blocking out things that do not serve you any purpose can also help you on this journey. Limiting contact with unnecessary people and things, and focusing only on the important things. Online shopping is a problem that many people are facing, especially in today's virtually stuck world- these things are artificial. Try to only shop for what you need, locally and in person rather than relying on online shopping. Being physically present might help you better understand the need for what you are getting and you may be able to better limit yourself rather than when it is online. When shopping, you should also try to use more cash and debit rather than credit. Another example of living within your means, advocates to not rack up debt for unnecessary things. That said, you should also learn to spend your money wisely. If your credit card is one that comes with benefits when used at grocery stores, then go ahead and rack it up. As long as you know you can pay it back in full on time, there is nothing wrong with letting your money that you were already going to spend come back to you in time. Being smart and being intentional should work together.

Another way to interpret living an intentional life could be to remain mindful with everything you do. Being aware that every little thing you do has a ripple effect that pours out into another section of your life and making it better is another example of leading by being intentional. Leading by this lifestyle may result in more gratitude and a refreshed attitude and outlook on life.

Setting Your Intentions

Now, how exactly do you go about setting intentions?

- Analyze your current stage. Write a detailed description of your financial means and how it affects your lifestyle both positively and negatively.

- Now, think about the choices you have made in the near or distant past that have contributed to the outcome we are facing today.

- Think about the lifestyle that you wish you had. What is included? A debt-free life? A six-figure income? It is important to make note of everything that comes to mind that you wish for yourself. Then, read the list out loud and rank them to you in importance using numbers.

- Pick the most important one from your top three. You cannot keep up with setting intentions for multiple things at once.

- Once you have picked the most important thing to you, go ahead and think about what it means to you. Then, think about what you would need or what you would need to change in order to obtain this goal you have written down. Use the manifestation technique if needed but for this exercise, you must map out using a timeline if you must- of what you need in order to get there. Be sure to only focus on the positives of this intention and not on any cons in order to gate out any negative energy that may be lurking.

Consider these steps when thinking about setting your intentions. It might take a while and you may not be able to decide on anything in one sitting. Allow yourself the time to consider the possible outcomes from this. Take several days if you need to and just consider the chapter as a whole. Discuss it with those closest to you and you can even cheat and ask them what they think your purpose in life is. The answer other people give you comes from an external point of view and they might point out something in you that you did not consider before.

We, as humans, are often terrible at criticizing and understanding ourselves and so it is alright to accept some help. It might be a good idea to ask this question to people of various roles in your life. For example, asking your mother, your sibling, your best friend, your coworker then your boss. Listen closely to what these people say about you. If you are someone who is impressionable by their environment like myself, you might be receiving all sorts of different answers- this is alright. If you are someone who seldom changes themselves, answers might tend to stay around the same area and that means you are very consistent and sure of yourself.

The Ideal You

You have completed many exercises now and have hopefully spent some time finding yourself and understanding what it means to be you. We hope we have put you in greater touch with your inner self in this book. Although we are thrilled that so many have benefited from our methods, we hope you will consider another one to determine the ideal image you have of yourself in your head.

You may need to dig a little deeper for this one and maybe even venture off into your earlier life to even begin understanding who you thought you would be. Or, maybe you have shifted into a person that you never thought you would be like. Or perhaps, you already are on track to becoming the most ideal version of yourself for you. In that case, congratulations. And on the off chance that you are still attempting to be the best you that you can be, follow along.

Many of us wish to be some extravagant or impossible persons when we grow up. From a princess to a fairy, all is possible in the mind of a child. However, as we get older these transition into more realistic goals such as astronauts, slowly making their way to the much more attainable careers such as lawyers or doctors. You may not have even reached goals but that is alright. Now the focus shifts to the financials and where you wish you were several years ago. Are you making as much as you were hoping you would? Well then, why are you not satisfied? Could it be because you are not actually making that much? Consider taxes and the number of expenses that are inherent with a larger income, or maybe you never made it there. Have no fear because the truth is most people have not made it there either.

Your ideal you is likely not the one to be stressed about money. Your ideal you probably does not live paycheck to paycheck or check their bank account before a trip to the grocery store. By focusing on the ideal you, spending is limited, money is put away into savings, and bills are taken care of with some money leftover to buy tequila shots on a Friday night out!

The barrier standing between you and your ideal self is well... you. As mentioned many times in this book, you cannot expect different outcomes with the same inputs. Consider your ideal self and her mindset. Would she agree with your decisions? Would she be making the same choices, going to the same places or hanging around the same people you are with at the moment? If the answer is not a yes, or is hesitant, you need to change your surroundings. The worst that can happen from improving your life is that you are at a happier place in the distant future.

CHAPTER 7

Wealth Stability

In this chapter we will talk about wealth stability. What exactly does it mean to achieve financial stability? You by no means need to be rich or make a ton of money in order to be financially stable. Stability comes from peace of mind and knowing how to spend your money, save your money and invest your money. These are the three key points to keep in mind when you think about your finances.

- How to spend your money
- How to save your money
- How to invest your money

You cannot skip one of these. Money is made to be spent and there will always be a reason for you to spend money. The trick is knowing when and where to spend it. Bills and payables must always be prioritized when your paycheck comes in. Debts, such as credit card bills will quickly pile up and leave you in an endless cycle of interest payments. Pay close attention to your spending on the card and be sure to limit spending above 10% of your limit to a minimum. Therefore, if your limit is $5,000 on your credit, do not spend more than $500 at one time before paying off the rest. Although it may seem harmless enough to do so, this may seriously lower your credit score, making it yet another great example of learning to live within your means.

An easy solution to this may be to open up many credit cards and use 10% on each card so as to not affect your credit score but this may also not be a good idea for your financial journey. More accounts just means more time and effort spent on keeping track, paying off and even worse building up points. As you should all know, never sign up for a credit card without benefits. Even if the money back is a small percentage, you may as well get enough money to get a free meal out of it. This is another example of letting your money work for you rather than working for your money. I have so far racked up enough points on my credit for about four round trip plane tickets. This was made by keeping one credit card with a high purchase limit and charging all possible charges to the same card. Most credit cards offer higher point levels for purchases on gas and groceries which is great because everyone needs to be fed and most people drive cars on fuel. Get into the habit of ditching the debit card that often charges you per use. Credit cards are a much less hassle, with much more benefits. Leave the negative stigma behind and remember you are a responsible adult being.

Saving your money is the next important thing to be aware of on our list. Saving is more important than spending and you should be wary of your purchases once you have hit your target for necessities, a topic covered more in-depth in Chapter 9. Saving for a reason such as a down payment on a car payment, or for absolutely no reason at all should be a practice in any household. It is understood that some homes survive by living from one paycheck to the next but it is time for those chains to be broken. Whether you have to pick up extra shifts or a side hustle, you need to be making more money than you are spending in any given situation.

In an ideal world, 20-30% of your income monthly should be deposited right into your savings without a need for the money. This is because once money is deposited into your savings, it should be erased from your memory. Whether you have a goal you plan to reach or are saving for a rainy day, your savings account should be untouchable. Once you establish a habit of digging into your savings with the slightest inconvenience, it will be a hard habit to break free from.

Preferably, you should open an investment savings account with your current bank. Most banks offer services as such where you can deposit a predetermined amount of money directly into this account. Usually referred to as a 'mutual fund' account, the money in this account is invested by the trusted cadre of employees at the bank into accounts they believe will be profitable. Most banks allow for the client to decide on the adjustable risk level of their account ranging from lowest risk to highest risk, which impacts the portfolio of investments and therefore affecting the return on investment from the said portfolio. Higher-risk portfolios will have higher payouts with the price of higher risk of losing more than you have invested. Be sure to ask lots of questions and read the fine print in this process. These accounts should be adjustable should you decide on a different level of risk or deposit more (or less) into the account weekly, bi-weekly or monthly. I recommend this account for saving, especially if you have the tendency to dip into your savings because, in order to withdraw money from this account, you must set up an account and wait around three business days for the transaction to take place. If you are lazy enough to turn to your savings, you will likely be too lazy to follow all these guidelines. Your money will be safe and will likely make you some money in the meantime while the dividends build up. Your savings are meant to be out of sight and certainly out of mind.

The last item on the list is investing your money. Although the mutual fund account mentioned above does a good job of investing your money for you, it is very minimal and not coming directly from you. This step is so important that even your savings account should be an investment account in disguise.

Most people usually think about the stock market when the topic of investing financially is brought up. While this is relevant, it is not necessarily the sole means of investing.

Investing can be done through many different methods. From the stock market to cryptocurrency to real estate, investing a way for your money to return to you in abundance without actual labor. Of course, that goes to say that it does not mean no work at all goes into this because it does. You must first figure out the type of investing that you will be partaking in. The three that I have listed are the most common ways and stock market investments and cryptocurrency are often employed together.

If you have decided to take your chance on the market, first do some research. Understand how the stock market works and key terms such as 'bear market' and 'bull market' and all other niches. It is a complicated place to be and so will usually take a couple of rounds of research to get it down. If you are a visual learner, we strongly recommend some great YouTube videos such as:

How Does the Stock Market Work? by Oliver Elfenbaum and Explained: The Stock Market as seen on Netflix but available on Youtube.

These videos do a wonderful job of explaining how the stock market works and attempt to put into simpler words an otherwise very complicated market.

Concluding your research, if you decide that the stock market appeals to you, you now must decide how much you are willing to invest. I strongly advise against investing all your savings or even any amount of your savings. Your investing and saving accounts should be different and serve different purposes. You will also interact more with your investment accounts than your savings accounts. Start off small and once you have enough, I would say a couple hundred is sufficient, now begin looking for applications that support investing. Wealthsimple is a very efficient and simple mobile app to use in this process. This particular app will help you keep track of your investments and also offer you an opportunity to dabble in cryptocurrency as well- at least two main ones consisting of Bitcoin and Ethereum.

You are also responsible for any tax purposes resulting from your adventures in investing. These applications may appear to be simple phone processes, but you are required to enter your Social Insurance Number and such before beginning your investment journey. Therefore, you are responsible for paying any taxes if you must have significant earnings. This also means that the government is able to keep track of your earnings from the stock market and any other similar investments. All income earned from such investments is indeed taxable.

While the stock market and cryptocurrency are some amazing ones to begin your investment journey with limited funds and a controlled environment, there are still other great ways to invest your money in the long run with a great return on investment. Real estate is one of the ways you suggest you do this. You will definitely need a lot more capital for these investments as opposed to entering the stock market. You will also need to do a lot more significant research as this investment will most likely cause you to spend hundreds of thousands of dollars.

First, begin your research into the housing market and understand how it works, how you become a homeowner and landlord as well as learning about the legal matters in your particular area. What are the responsibilities of a residential and business landlord, then decide which direction is best suited for you. After your initial research and once you have gained enough insight into the workings of real estate and the market, begin looking for those trends, such as bubbles within the area you wish to invest your money into. Notice any trends or establishments in the area that may increase or decrease the market value of homes in the near future. Then, reach out to a local real estate agent and begin your search.

Whether you are currently renting and wish to become a first-time homeowner or if you are a current homeowner and are looking for more rental properties, one should always aim to keep up with developments in real estate. You will likely need to put around a five percent to 20% down payment when making the purchase, then analyze your contract for the mortgage to decide what is the best for you regarding interest rates and types. Also, be sure to put the time and effort in to find out the banks and credit unions that offer the best interest because it may not be the bank you deal with at the moment. Once you have done your research, studied the market and saved your money, you can now make your purchase.

The point of any of your investments is to generate income revenue for yourself. The purpose or mission of this particular investment is to buy a home when the market is down and buy with confidence. Once you have bought your property, you can now choose to live in it as a homeowner, and pay off your mortgage and sell it in the future for a profit. You can also choose to buy it and once it is fixed up, sell it for profit as well (minus the expenses and time spent on fixing it up). Or, you can choose to buy the property and list it as a rental and find a suitable renter. Be sure to conduct thorough background and credit checks as well as confirmation of their I.D. and employment. You can then rent out the improved property for a couple hundred more than what the mortgage is per month. This definitely requires a lot of time and attention and can be considered a part-time job and the house will still need constant maintenance.

Now that you are informed of all the ways to wisely spend your money to make money in the long run, you need to make the decision for yourself based on your own preferences and means. Be sure to not put yourself in a position that places you in further debt you cannot afford, or dive straight into a risky pool. Moderation and knowledge are key when dealing with investments. Be sure to always conduct relevant and specific research.

Relationship With Money

If you are a reader, I think it is safe to assume your relationship with money could use some improvement. Whichever way it may bend, it is important to recognize healthy habits when handling money.

Money is meant to be spent and while it is important to keep this in mind and not be in a constant state of panic over saving, it is also essential that money does not just flow through you. Moderation is the key to your happiest lifestyle. Growing up with a lot of money, you may be used to certain luxuries and not think twice about blowing half your paycheck on a dinner. Now, becoming more financially independent, that behavior needs to be recognized as harmful and causing a bad relationship with money. On the contrary, being raised in a poorer environment, maybe it is your desire without knowing to hoard all the money you make so that you can be prepared for anything. This is, once again, deemed undesirable behavior when trying to establish a stable financial presence.

Do not try to hoard and save all your money, and do not get caught up in spending it as you make either. Instead, find the true balance between both. Spend your money in ways that make you happy at the right time and places. Although you might disagree, you do not need to be spoiled every day or every week. Celebrating small achievements by yourself by treating yourself to something you have wanted is alright. Your money will do you no good stashed in a safe either. You should be okay with spending it on you and your loved ones as you cannot be buried with it. A better way to do this might be to just discover better and non-monetary rewards for yourself. Instead of spoiling yourself to a new bag after a rough week at work, consider just taking the day off next week or reward yourself by taking on less than the usual at work to allow yourself to bounce back properly.

Changing the way you view rewards will truly be an ally to you on your quest to financial stability and relationship with money. Even though it seems corny and unlikely now, the best thing you can do for yourself is to adjust yourself to think that fitness related things are rewards for you. Going on runs, yoga classes, and Pilates lessons should slowly start becoming a part of your life and in turn, become more valuable than other things. Once your body is beginning to get into better shape, you will automatically find yourself changing other aspects of your life as well. When I first began working out, it was for the sole purpose of losing weight. I then began regularly working out, which made me naturally get tired earlier and wake up earlier. I then began realizing that what I am eating and what I am doing contradict each other and my progress was cancelling out. And so, I changed my regimen, experimented with different diets and eventually stopped eating out and found foods that worked best for me. Then, I started reading fitness and mediation books which rekindled my love for reading and I started reading my favorite fantasy books again. I quickly noticed that I was becoming so much more disciplined in so many areas than one by deciding to make just one change to my life.

And so, everything in your life, including your relationship with money is a total ripple effect that overflows into other parts of your life. Being more self-aware and disciplined in one area leads you to be more attentive in others. As the example goes with the one decision to lose weight and become more active, my entire way of life changed in a matter of months. Making the decision to become better takes one second. It takes a couple weeks to build a new habit. Then, the rest will follow. Pick up a new habit that is going to change your lifestyle every week. Pick up a new one until you see all your old ones perish and your entire life is changed. A chain reaction is the best thing that can happen in your life when you are trying to change it.

Keep in mind the importance of balance and that if you are able to manage your time and money wisely, you will eventually cover all your bases and afford your needs as well as your wants. It does not happen overnight but once you can master the three categories as mentioned above consisting of saving, investing and spending, you are on your way to a better you!

Setting Yourself Up for Success

Now, all of the above we have been discussing is always easier said than done. Telling someone who has never been concerned with finances to begin saving their money, or someone who is not comfortable spending to begin investing is a tough ask. However, you need to change your mindset in order to change your lifestyle.

What does setting yourself up for success look like financially? It looks like someone who is not afraid of taking risks while taking careful precautions. It also looks like someone who does a considerate amount of research and takes in all feedback before deciding to make any major or small changes to their finances. Knowledge of what you're doing may make some decisions easier for you. For example, investing in a cryptocurrency without any prior knowledge is foolish. However, if you take your time to watch videos, read articles, listen to qualified and knowledgeable persons and follow trends, you will likely feel a lot more confident in your decision to invest. This is normal and should be conducted with any and all decisions in life. Doing your research will also take some pressure off your shoulders if you are someone who struggles when making decisions, especially financial ones.

Personally, I am the type of person who carefully weighs all risks before agreeing to enter into them. I bring a $20 bill with me to the casino on a night out and make a deal with myself prior to not spending a dollar more than what I am entering with. I then use my $20 to play a game of my choice and if I win, I am very happy. If I lose, I consider the $20 the price of my entertainment for the night and leave the casino feeling alright. This is a great exercise to try if you are someone who struggles to take risks or someone who takes too many unnecessary risks. Being disciplined enough to keep the promises you have made to yourself is a sure way to adjust how you make decisions in other big picture situations.

Setting yourself up for success and becoming the best you that you can be is as simple as becoming educated. Doing your research and expanding your information bank will be your true allies on your personal wealth journey.

CHAPTER 8

Investing in Yourself

We have touched bases on investing your money and taking care of your finances. Now, we move on to ways that you can begin investing in yourself. At the end of the day, you are the one making your money, spending it and investing it. You decide what you do with your money and the more you feel better about it and are more informed in your decisions, the better for you and your wealth.

And while there are fewer guides to this directly; this part is better to be taken care of personally. Investing in yourself takes many different forms and self-care does not have to be the main point. Investing in yourself can mean job searching when you are unhappy at your current job, changing routines when you are not seeing results and taking care of your mind and body so you may better operate yourself. You may also notice a change in your finances as this happens, whether this is in the form of a better paying job with better conditions or the latter, once you invest in yourself and make the conscious decision to better yourself, the rest will follow. Manifestation needs to be mentioned.

While some suggestions to investing in yourself involve making some major changes to things that no longer serve a purpose to you, it can virtually mean anything. Investing in yourself varies from person to person and can be as simple as changing the brand of your shampoo to one that is gentler on your hair. For these purposes, we would like to focus more on the financial and the overall health of the reader. Some things to consider when beginning to invest in yourself is to consider things that are no longer interesting to you and things you are no longer passionate about. As mentioned earlier, it is often the place you spend the most of your time and energy at- work. Take a minute to think about your place of employment, your co-workers, supervisors and the actual work that you perform. Ask yourself if you are still passionate about the organization and if your values still match up enough for you to enjoy your time there.

Outside of work, it is also important to invest your time into the right people as well. You are a reflection of the people you hang around even if you think that might not apply to you. Your friends, your coworkers and everyone in between influence your life more than you think. Investing your time into people who are doing better than you so that you may be able to learn from them and elevate to their level is one of the best things you can do for yourself. Do not let yourself become a product of your environment or your social circle. It will certainly not be easy to cut off the people who have been in your life for years, but changing your lifestyle is never easy.

Change your mindset then your lifestyle. If others cannot keep up then it is time to move on. Attracting what is meant for you through manifestation as we have mentioned might also work for people as well.

As you move on up in life, you should aim to befriend and associate with people who are doing better than you. Dragging you down is not an option. Hang around places that you are trying to become a part of. Drop your friends who do nothing but party and bring you into the environment, and swap them out for friends you meet in your cycle class so that you can be more active and productive.

Another aspect of your life to consider should be what you do with your free time. The book has already spoken some about habits and building better ones but these activities should also aim to better yourself as well. Maybe taking up workshops or lectures can be a good place to start. Taking the time to educate yourself further in your field, your hobbies or financially will help you expand your mindset and become a better person in the long run. The need and feel to expand should always remain a part of you in anything that you do.

When on your way to discovering new hobbies, consider adapting ones that add an intellectual aspect to your life. Whether it be reading, writing or taking on a whole new skill, constant research and updating your skills should be the most important part of it. As mentioned in the earlier chapters, never be satisfied with where you are. When you have mastered one skill, take on another one. Once you have finished all the books in your personal collection, start another collection. There is always something you have not done and a skill you have not perfected. A well-rounded person is who one should aspire to be. Be a little knowledgeable in all things rather than a lot knowledgeable in a couple things. This will make for a more interesting life.

Bettering and investing yourself has to be done through the betterment of your soft skills as well. While picking up a new trade is exciting, improving your social skills, networking and multi-tasking are also an important part in your evolution. The ways to improve these skills can be through taking on more risks socially, not avoiding social interactions, taking on more responsibilities and interacting more with people. The more you can spend time with others and get to know them, the more empathetic you can be, the more networking you can get done and the more you can learn from their experiences.

The saying 'networking and who you know will get you through doors that your degree cannot' is very much true. You have a better chance at landing a job, getting into a program or obtaining a position if someone you know is already connected in the field. While it may not seem fair, life hardly ever is. Focus on expanding your network and connecting with people who are in positions that you are working towards. Connect with your boss and his friends. Do not ever say no to an office party, lunch with coworkers or any other event that may seem to be socially motivated within the professional setting. A lot more business talks go down at these places than you would think. Oftentimes women are excluded from the boys' club events such as going golding on the weekend or trying a new BBQ place during lunch. Make a bigger effort as a woman to be included because these boys will not invite you ever. You need to establish yourself as a valuable person who needs to be included. This is certainly painfully to write out as a true feminist but you have got to call if like you see it.

Another thing to keep an eye out for when looking to expand your network are community events. There may be places you do not expect such as professional seminars and things of the same nature. These things are usually by invitation so you may have to work a little harder to be invited, but it will surely be worth it in the end if you can meet your mentor or your next employer at one of these events. You can also benefit from changing the places of your leisure. Hanging around higher end bars and restaurants and country clubs can certainly put you in touch with higher end people. For example, if you are in finance looking to get your foot in the door with Wall Street, then try grabbing lunch at restaurants in the area, the bars and such. Hang around people and places that the better you would be hanging out at. You do not have to wait to be better to act better. The more confidence you have, the more people will already believe it, and so will you.

You Are Worth More Than You Think

Investing in yourself might seem to be unnecessary and easily dismissed by most since we are conditioned to think that we will always be fine. This is a terrible mindset and should be abolished and instead replaced with a train of thought that reminds you that you only get one of yourself. Place self-care a little higher on your list and begin investing in yourself.

Other than being employed in a field you are passionate about with a company that aligns with your values, you also need to pay attention to your work-life balance as well. It is easy to get carried away with work and give it more than you should when you are passionate but remember that you are an employee. Remember that should you no longer be a part of that organization, you would be very easily replaced within a week. This is not to say that you should not give your all to your work, but also remember that you need to take care of yourself as well.

Mentally and physically, being more aware of how you are treating yourself can open more doors for you to do better at doing so. Recognizing harmful patterns that are interfering with you becoming the best version of yourself must be recognized before they can ever be eliminated. Investing time into yourself means taking the time to spend it to find yourself and what works for you. Whether it be mental, physical, spiritual or emotional, you need to make sure that you are paying attention to your needs simultaneously.

For this exercise, it is once again a thinker. Find a spot where you are comfortable and get ready to become vulnerable. Think about all the things that you do in your daily life. From the moment you wake up to the moment that you fall asleep. Matter of fact, consider those parts of your life too. The pillow you put your head on and the mattress that's under you. How does everything feel to begin with? Then, think about your actions. The first thing you do when you get up from your sleep, and everything that follows it. Try to time how much time you spend on each activity including your phone, exercise and cooking. Differentiate between habits and things you have to put effort into at this time, and then consider things that you wish were habits but are not.

Now, throughout your day, what does not feel good, and what could be improved? You are and will always be your best and greatest investment and should be treated as such. If anything does not feel good, it should be replaced with something better. For example, if you do not get a good night's sleep due to your mattress situation, consider getting a new one. These things are important for your long-term health and the decisions you make in your daily life and as we know now, the decisions you make in life are the most important things you will do. We make tens of thousands of choices in a day from what side of the bed we wake up onto the way we take our eggs in the morning. Being aware that you are constantly making decisions might guide you to think more about them and make better choices moving forward.

Other ways to take care and invest in yourself can include letting yourself venture and take more chances and risks in life. As an adult, you probably dismiss a lot of thoughts in your head because you think you do not have the money or the time or the resources to make something come true. I say, forget all of that! Be impulsive and spontaneous for a change, and live in the feeling. If I have a thought in my head, no matter if the sky comes down, it is getting done within the day. Nothing can stop me from making my idea come to life once I have it- try that more often. If you want to add a slide to your pool, screw being too old, go ahead and order one. You are never going to be any younger than you were when you first thought of it. Money spent on these types of things is money spent to invest in yourself. While it is important to not get carried away, the once in a while spoiling yourself thing we spoke about earlier in the text can be applied here. Spoil yourself by making one of your spontaneous thoughts come true and letting your inner child free. These types of purchases are ones that will not only live in your memories forever, but also heal a part of you that you might not have known healing from another time in your life. It is often hard to reconnect with a lost part of yourself so if you have a feeling, just run with it. Invest everything in yourself and reap the fruit of your labor.

Other than that, being mindful of your activities when you are not working, such as exercising and reading and being more knowledgeable are also ways to invest in yourself. Take up hobbies, rekindle all things you love to do and be sure to spend at least an hour a day with a person that you love. The success and the thrill of it all are always more enjoyable when you have someone else to share the experience with. The peace of mind that comes with financial stability should also be stable. You should be appreciative of the moment while working towards more but never to the point of exhausting yourself.

Mindfulness and Letting Go

Circling back to being mindful, letting go is also a big part of personal growth. Whether it be implied to your personal life and relationships, your career or your finances, it is important to not latch onto things longer than you should. Should you invest and lose money as one does at times, or not make as much as you would have liked, take the time to feel the disappointment and the regret for about 10 seconds, countdown and then let it go.

There truly is no inconvenience in life so great for you to dwell longer than 10 seconds on it. Sure, things happen and things go wrong all the time and your best bet then is to understand what happened, why it happened and deciding it will never happen again, or how it will happen differently. Being mindful is just that. Understanding that things happen, staying in the present without disconnecting or disassociating and dealing with things as they come. Handling things as they happen to you and not allowing them to partake in parts of your life that they should not be is an essential part of being mindful. Be present, practice your breathing and visualize everything.

Let us practice a mediation session. Find a preferably darker and quiet room in your home or somewhere you feel safe and free from distraction or disturbance. Make yourself comfortable. It is best if you are able to take on a criss cross type seating position on the floor- try to avoid any soft places to sit. Once you are comfortable enough, begin breathing in through your nose and out through the mouth. Take your time when breathing and really focus on it. Imagine the air coming into your body from your nose and filling up your lungs with air, then letting go of it just as it came in all the same. Now, on your own time you can begin to close your eyes while still practicing breathing. At this time, try to visualize your breath. From the color to the smell to the feeling of it, attempt to visualize it in your head as accurately as possible. Visualize your breath going all around your body now, not just your lungs. Your whole body is being filled up with strong, fresh air and cleansed because of it. When you are imagining this, do a mental scan of your whole body from the top of your head to your toes. Think about how each inch of your body feels and how the breathing is affecting the way your body is. Try to identify if there is a particular spot of your body that feels a little off or hurts. This might be due to some muscle tension and you can focus on being aware of it, massaging it and letting the pain and feeling flow through you until it is no longer there.

At this point of the exercise, try to think about all the little things that happened to you the past day or the past week that you really did not appreciate. Try to imagine the exact way those situations made you feel and why they made you feel like that. Pinpoint the exact feeling and minute these things happened. Now, think about all possible outcomes that can happen within the given scenarios. Consider then how you acted. Imagine you have been given a do over in all of these cases. Play out in your head what you would have done knowing what you know now and the state of mind you are in now. If you would have done something different, think about why that may be and how to ensure your actions match the person you are meant to be. If you would have acted the same way, you may need to continue this exercise until your answer changes, or maybe you have reacted the exact right way.

Everything should be flowing through you. By now, you understand the importance of doing your research before proceeding with anything and should take that advice with you everywhere you go. And so, if you had the correct intentions going into this journey, you did your proper research and checked off all the boxes, there really is not much more you can do. Life comes in waves and you cannot always expect to ride them.

CHAPTER 9

Spending Plan

Now, creating a spending plan is essential. What should your spending plan consist of? It should include all of your expenses for the month, for example. Here is a list of things to consider when creating a plan:

- Rent/Mortgage and all other housing expenses
- Utilities (heating/ cooling/ hydro/ electricity etc...)
- Bills (phone bill/ landline/ TV etc...)
- Subscriptions (Netflix/ Apple Music/ Amazon etc…)
- Groceries
- Car Payments
- Insurance
- Gas and Car Maintenance
- Contingencies such as emergency funds
- Investing Portfolio
- Savings Accounts
- Retirement Funds

Review this list and think about the amount of money spent on the listed categories. You can replace some if they do not apply to you. For example, if you do not currently own a car, replace the car payments with other transportation expenses such as your bus pass or the amount dedicated to your Uber rides.

Now, get to work and list everything out for you to see on paper. Do one for weekly and one for monthly. You may want to employ the use of a free software such as Microsoft Excel at this time. Review your list and highlight the categories that are eating up a majority of your income and see if those things are recurring and/or necessary. Most people will find their housing expenses is the most expensive thing on their list and this will likely remain this way until you have paid off the mortgage on your own home or of course, move back in with the parents but no one likes to admit that level of defeat.

Next, focus on things that should not be on your lists such as takeout food and driving services. You are already spending money on groceries and likely throw out a portion of your fridge out regularly. Or, opt out of insurance, driving services and car payments by taking public transportation if you can- especially if you live in the city. Try to minimize all of your fixed and variable costs wherever you can.

Fixed costs are costs that will remain the same throughout the period of time you are paying them for. For example, your mortgage, insurance, and phone bill are all examples of fixed costs for the most part. The amount you pay stays the same over time and will not change. You can expect these payments to be recurring regularly and these are likely things that may be necessary. Variable costs are costs that change over time and are not guaranteed to remain the same or even occur every time. While your base phone plan may be the same every month and therefore fixed, the pay per use data part of your bill is varied since the amount of data you use and therefore pay for is changed over time. Variable costs should be a little easier to control and eliminate. The amount spent on food, entertainment, clothing and miscellaneous items are considered variable costs since they tend to change from month to month.

While creating your spending plan, be sure to identify which category your costs and expenses fall under. Every cost you can eliminate is another dollar you can invest into your future. Be extra wary of variable costs that tend to occur every month with different amounts when they really should not be such as clothing. No one person needs to order clothing for themselves every month. Be sure to be on the hunt for sale items, coupon codes and seasonal discounts when shopping and try to purchase items that are not too trendy as they will likely only be worn for a season. If you spend too much on gas, try to cut down on your joy rides and so on.

Your spending plan is for your own reference and should be completely honest. You need to list all your expenses at face value so you can seriously review and analyze your spending to find patterns and benefit yourself. Being honest with yourself is the first step to improving your lifestyle. If you are attempting to try these exercises with your partner, or have a case of the joint bank accounts, conduct these activities separately on your own time then come together later with broad categories such as food, clothing and entertainment rather than specific stores and orders.

And while most married couples choose to combine their finances, in this book and context, we strongly advise against this. It is much easier and more beneficial to keep finances separate to keep track and also to fall back on in case of emergency or unforeseen circumstances. This is assuming that both partners generate income, but should still be considered with homemakers as well.

For the next part of your spending plan, consider your income and separate it into blocks. Start with bigger chunks and then split them into smaller slices of a pie. These can be done online quite easily over applications such as Microsoft Excel or Google Charts, or any other free online software program. Of course, drawing is just as effective. First, conduct the chunks for what your current spending looks like. Then, make one that represents the spending plan that you wish you were following. Color code them if possible then compare them to each other. What are the differences? Are the savings chunks bigger in your desired plan as opposed to your current one? Is the housing chunk significantly smaller? What can you do to try to get as close to your desired pie chart as possible? Brainstorm all possible replacements to your current expensive spending habits and any other similar activities that require less capital or cause less of a financial burden. While your spending plan should aim to minimize costs while maximizing savings, you should not sacrifice your hobbies and things that make you happy and the person you are (unless your hobby is gambling).

Be sure that you are being honest and give thought to your spending plan. A lot of people will lie to themselves in order to seem better in their heads. Put together your spending plan alone and be sure to include everything that you spend your income on. Do not minimize some spending or maximize the usual amount you set aside for the good things like savings and investments. Lay it all upfront so that you can understand better and be more wary of where your money accurately goes.

Your spending plan is not the same as an expense plan. Focus only on things you tend to spend money on in your average life. We will put together a personal expense report further into the book once you have had practice analyzing your spending and putting together a general list. Expense reports are more detailed and require a lot more attention to detail and mathematics than a personal spending plan.

For the best results, be sure to update your spending plan as your life continues to change and evolve. Do not keep the same spending plan for more than six months because think about how much your life adjusts and changes in a matter of half of a year. From your revenue streams to your expenses, these things will likely change a couple times in a span of a year, especially if you are young or a student. Your income should always be on the rise or you should always be looking for more ways to make it higher while also trying to bring down expenses as much as you can.

Setting Goals

Now that you have laid out your spending plan and were able to carefully analyze and identify patterns, we are ready to give meaning to our exercises. Setting goals is a crucial part of your financial journey and ensuring that you are on track to becoming a better you. When creating your spending plan, think about all the things that you wish to have accomplished in the near future, then your long-term plans. Consider the barriers that are standing in between you and the said goals. These are achievements that should be of the greatest priority to you and little things that stand in your way such as saving more or having a better handle on your finances should be eliminated.

Physically write out all the goals you have set for yourself. Begin with your end goal. Although the most epic of all goals, it needs to be addressed first as every other decision and goal will be connected to the ultimate end goal. Think about how you see yourself in retirement and the lifestyle that you have. Did you save enough for retirement to live alright, or are you running your own business on the side? Did you leave your business to your kids or are you receiving benefits from the company you worked for 40 years at? Be quite specific with your vision. Write all the details down and really imagine you are living that life.

Then, write out all that you wish to achieve in the next 10 years. Imagine yourself at your job. What kind of position are you in and what kind of company are you working for? Are you happy at your job or are you on the hunt for a new one? Are you employed at all or running your own business at this time? Now think about your home and social life. Imagine you own your own home and a summer home with no to minimal debt and your dream car. Imagine a position that allows you to not bring work home and pay you a fair wage for your work while also valuing you as a person and allowing you to have more autonomy at your job. Think about all the promotions you must have gotten and will continue to receive. Once again, be very specific in your imaginary scenario and attempt to write it all down. Now, move on to your goals for the next year or so and this is where it should begin to get more specific. Think about your life in its entirety within a year and include professional and social achievements you wish to achieve in that timespan.

Once all these are written, be sure to date them and store them away for safekeeping in a spot where they will be free from damage but also can be accessible to remind yourself constantly. Framing them or taping a laminated version on the fridge seem to be good ideas.

Achieving Goals

You have now set some serious goals for yourself to achieve in your lifetime but you are not done. While you have thought long and hard and established some goals for yourself, it is now time to set them. You can do this by setting even more recent goals and allowing yourself to celebrate the smaller accomplishments.

As a person who must operate on a to-do list, I have quite a few running at all times. I keep a personal agenda for my monthly appointments, birthdays, reminders and big picture things. I have all my electronic calendars combined for all my work and personal calendars to be combined into one place as well. This way, not only will i have written down my plans physically for me to remember, but I also receive reminders on my phone and laptop prior. A definite lifesaver to get that 30-minute check in notification before a meeting you almost forgot about.

On top of all this, you should also keep a daily list as well. I do this by the most efficient method of using a whiteboard. A small whiteboard works and it is used to write all of your goals for the day, updated every night before sleep. This should involve the most mundane of tasks, from practicing yoga in the morning to checking your emails. Of course, exclude things such as eating or sleeping, but you can keep things such as making your bed and vacuuming and such under the general category of cleaning. As you go about your day and perform these acts, cross them off one by one. This will give you a great sense of achievement and push yourself to become the best of yourself and make that whiteboard look brand new by the end of the day.

While it may seem to deviate from the point, keeping tabs on yourself and setting certain goals to accomplish is a great way to keep yourself accountable. As well, all the little things that you achieve are a great proof of your self-discipline and will continue to develop. The little things that you do are also likely to be working towards the bigger goals you have set for yourself. For example, I am sure you imagine yourself fit and healthy in 20 years, and writing 'yoga' and 'skincare' on your daily whiteboard will only set yourself up for success in the future.

Before you know it, you will be reading to yourself the goals you have set all those years ago and thanking yourself for building the discipline and work ethic to stick to it and make it happen.

For some, it might not work to keep tabs on yourself. Some people do not have the commitment levels nor the discipline to hold themselves accountable. If you are one of these people who will set goals for themselves all the time to never achieve them and leave them where they are, you may want to consider going public. Going public by posting your goals on social media should hold you more accountable for the goals you set and the timeframe you do it in. It might also help you to make your goals a little bit more realistic as well. Now, this is not to say that every little goal and daily task should be televised, but certain bigger goals might be better to do so.

For example, if your goal is to lose 30 pounds by summer and you have set that goal for yourself and yet find yourself constantly snacking on food and not working out, maybe it is time to speak your goal into existence. Post it on social media for all of your friends and family and associates to see. Make a post that specifically states you will lose 30 pounds by the end of June. Then, record yourself at the moment and take a picture of your starting weight. You do not need to share this right now, or ever. Then, remember that people saw this and begin working on yourself. You might find an extra burst of energy you did not think possible. Once you think you have reached your goal or exceeded it, now you can take another video or picture and visually record your new goal weight. You can choose to share either the before and after progress pictures or just your after progress and let people know that you stuck to your goal and made it. People will love to celebrate your achievement with you.

Thus, the best way to achieve goals is to literally hold yourself accountable for all goals that you set. Whether it is physically writing them down for yourself or exposing yourself to the world, it's important to keep track. There is no better feeling than when you get to reach and celebrate when you reach your goals. Keep that in mind as much as possible and never allow yourself to give up on yourself.

CHAPTER 10

Leverage

You have now mastered mindfulness, your purpose and how to use your money the best way to serve your needs and wants. The next thing you need to learn how to operate is to leverage your capital and resources to best serve your needs.

In this text, we will use the word leverage to describe the best possible situation for you to be in financially or otherwise. Leveraging where you are at the moment means to pull yourself up by the ropes and discover heights you have not experienced before. Leveraging your money is divided into debits and credits. Your debits will be things you are bringing in money from such as your income, your side hustle and tour investments. On the other hand, credits will be things that your debits are being spent on such as car notes, housing payments and anything else that require you to make a payment out of your bank account.

Identifying the two categories might help you better understand your finances and if needed, create a balance sheet for yourself. While not many people are experienced or even understand what an expense report is or looks like, creating one for yourself by setting up debit and credit accounts may suit your needs. To get started, let's circle back to our earlier activities. As discussed in earlier chapters, consider everything from big to small that you make your income on. Ideally, this expense report will be created monthly so even things such as the $10 your friend gave you for gas should be reported as a debit. As well, all little expenses from the flowers you have bought yourself to the ice cream you decided to pick up on the way home, should be included in your credits. This will give you a much better idea on what you spend your money on monthly. As well, at the end of your expense report, your debits and credits should match to the same amount. This can be done through not only considering all expenses but your savings accounts as well.

If for whatever reason your debits and credits do not match up to equal amounts at the end of the day, is it because of an abundance of debits or too many credits? If the answer is an abundance of debits, this is a good problem to have. This means that you are making more than you are spending. We fix this on an expense report by spending more, but not really. Instead of having leftover debits and spending more, try adding more money into your investments or your savings accounts. If your problem is having too many credits, this is a harder problem to fix and means you are not making enough money. Spending more than you make is a sure way to pile on the debt that is sure to become unmanageable as time goes on. This certainly takes more time and effort to correct and the only way to do is by dabbling in new ways to bring in money. Whether through a better job, picking up some small jobs or investing your money better, your debits can be increased by making more money than you already make.

Consider all your costs and the hidden costs you do not usually think about. Circling back to the example of a friend paying you $10 for gas, this is a hidden cost if not discussed. If you carpool on your way to work and pick up a friend who lives 15 minutes away all week (five days a week) for going to work and coming home, that equals up to a lot more than $10 a month for gas. Not a direct expense, but surely an expense either way, driving 30 minutes out of your way every day you work is a great way to empty your tank. Consider instead of entering a deal where they drive one week and you the next or setting up weekly payments that fairly represent the amount of gas your car is using up on your commutes. Do this for all other aspects of your expenses from weekly brunches with bottomless mimosas to turning on the heater for your pool every summer. When trying to become financially literate and responsible, all is fair game.

Of course, this goes without saying that all financial advice we give should be considered from person to person and should not interfere with your life so much to make it any less enjoyable. If asking for gas money will affect your friendships that you wish not to, or if cutting off the ice cream you get every Wednesday on your way home from work makes you happy, go for it. Be financially responsible and aware but also do not forget to also live life while doing so.

So then, how exactly can you leverage in such situations? Leveraging basically means being better off or just being better than what you would have considered fine. Having your debits empower your credits is one way of doing this. Another way is to just become more knowledgeable, free of things that do not benefit you and continue on your path to building up your savings. Starting up a 401k is leveraging yourself from now until your future. Investing your money leverages yourself for the near future and so forth.

As mentioned several times earlier in the text, it is important to keep in mind your future and how your future self would feel if your decision went one of the two ways. Consider the liabilities and the level of affect your decision would have. Even becoming more knowledgeable and informed with using technology is a great way to leverage yourself in the future and likely in the workplace as well. Consider the skills you wish to have and the skills your ideal self would have. Work on them. If you are a current human resources administrator but wish to become an accountant now, consider taking some classes for accounting, attending workshops and studying for your accounting license. Hard work takes time but all the time and effort put into yourself now will only make yourself work less in the future. Do not overlook the power of putting in time for yourself and letting yourself become the best version of you. The current you now might not have accomplished the things you have wished but you in the future will, thanks to the things you do now.

The next little bit of this chapter will speak on how to put together an expense sheet. Although the steps will describe it to be for use on the virtual web, it is very possible to put together an expense report with pen and paper. There are a number of applications that offer templates and help for free, but it is also alright to keep it old school as well. Read the next little bit carefully to soak in all the steps to putting together a standard personal expense report.

To put together a proper expense sheet, first pick out the software you wish to use. One of the most commonly used ones are Microsoft Excel and Vertex 42. While these are common, there are plenty of other free options available you can reach through the use of a Google search. Once you have established your platform, you are going to need to mark some identifiers. Templates found online can be misleading for this little bit as they are often used for businesses and not for personal use. For these purposes, our columns will include the date of the debit or credit, the place or use for it, the account it has gone into or come out of and the exact cost of the item or service. If you would like, you can also include another column meant for notes as you go along. These notes can include any relevant information related to the specific transaction from the reason for it to any other details that may be needed into the future. If you are someone who regularly makes similar purchases, for example grabbing a coffee on the way to work or paying for parking at a place you visit a couple times a week, it may be easier to break debits and credits into categories such as 'Coffee' or 'Car Expenses'. If you can do this, the list can include everything instead of being listed individually just be wary of your math at this step.

Remember that these expense reports are a lot more in need of detail than the spending plan we have put together. Your expense report should leave no room for assumption or guesswork and all your math and expenses must be exact. Do not round your numbers for nicer looking ones. What you see is what you get. This might be easier done if you are someone who keeps receipts instead of tossing them. Not only will this allow you to refer when you are unsure, but also in case of any return or warranty emergencies as well. Staple them if needed and dedicate a shoebox or filing system to your receipts. Being organized is another way to leverage yourself from now to the future.

When all your debits have been stated on the left side and all your receipts on the right, it is now time to add them all up. Like mentioned earlier, it is essential that your math be very exact in this process since we are trying to match up the debits and credits. Once you have your total for your debits, and your total for your credits, the two totals should equal each other to the cent. If not, you have done something wrong and should revisit your expense report and perhaps with someone else who can provide feedback or has some experience in bookkeeping.

Another way to leverage yourself is to consider finding a mentor. Someone who is experienced and, in the field, and success level you want to be in someone you should seek. Given my experience with mentors, they are often more excited than you and will offer any and all resources at their disposal to you. People are excited to share their information and knowledge with you and to help you achieve things in life. Maybe they want it for selfish reasons and to brag when taking credit but as long as you get where you are going, do not sweat the rest.

With this mentor, try to get them as close to yourself as possible. An older version of you would be preferred. They will have faced the same barriers or perks and can give you greater insight on how to overcome or properly utilize them. With this mentor, you can talk to them about all sorts of challenges and reach solutions with them. I have been employed as an administrative director at a renowned mentorship service and we have set up a plan with each mentor and mentee relationship that begins with them setting a beginning goal and meeting about twice before speaking about the goal. Discussing how far they have come, how they have got there and where to go from there. Once your hard work pays off and you have reached your goal, it is time to celebrate. But not for long. Once one goal is reached, it is time to set out for a new one. Your job is not done until you can truly say you will not improve from where you are now and that should be never!

Debits

When thinking about debits, consider every revenue of income you have. This category not only includes your salary, but quite literally anything that has brought capital into your banking accounts- cash or not. Even an e-transfer from a past expense should be considered when making this list. For our non-accounting purposes, debits will stay as things that are bringing in money to your accounting and therefore increasing your net worth rather than things that are decreasing your liabilities such as paying off debt.

Write all relevant income sources down on one side of the paper, being sure to separate the paper down the half evenly. Although we recommend using one of the above mentioned softwares for this purpose, a handwritten expense report is just as effective. It may also be a good idea to draft it up by hand before deciding to transfer it to your software as well. Be sure to separate them into the categories they need to be in if they are constant and recurring more than once. There is no need for clutter in an expense report.

Credits

Credits are anything that transfers money out of your account. Your debits are spent on your credits and quite literally so. While your debts do not fit into either debit or credits, they still exist and have certainly been thought of. For your debt you have paid off for the month, record them under credits. If you are under greater debt that has not allowed you to repay it in full, create a category under the name of accounts payable. Now, under this category, include only debt that you have racked up this month that you intended to pay back in full or in part next month. Your shopping spree on the credit card can be seen here. However, do not include debts that you have no intention or means to pay back in the near future/ next month. These included car notes and mortgages. Record the exact amount you pay every month under credits but not the entirety of the debt.

Although in accounting, credits would not include things that decrease liabilities, for our purposes, they do. We are keeping it very simple and since paying off debt requires us to physically take money out of our account to pay it off, it is now considered a credit. This should not affect the overall purpose of your personal expense sheet.

One thing about credits that you should keep an eye out for is that they should always remain lower than your debits. No matter which way you decide to spend your money or expenses, credits are things that drain your account and your account should never be drained faster than it is being filled. Even when paying off debts, you should never spend more than you are making. You will only enter into more debt. There is also an art to paying off debt anyway. Know that you can pay something off in full, but do not do so. When you purchase something with a credit card, play it to your advantage in order to receive the best possible credit score you can. Pay off half of your debt on the card when you initially make the purchase. Do not pay off the other half, but rather wait until about three days before the minimum due date, or the grace period ends then pay off the rest.

The grace period on a credit card is the time that the bank will allow you to borrow the money before they begin charging interest. More often than not, you can expect the grace period to be around 21 days from the date you make the purchase. And although the interest rate may differ from one bank to the next, it will likely be around the ballpark of 19.99%. Be sure to look at all the details that come with the fine print when you are making the decision to be a credit card holder. While there are a lot of rewards and cash back opportunities that are being offered, keep in mind that banks are indeed a business and have to make money somehow. You will not receive a reminder to pay back your loan and will be automatically charged the amount when your grace period is up.

One way to make sure that you are not missing these deadlines and are keeping a proper track of your purchases is to stick with one bank and one credit card. Two at max. If you do not have too many personal expenses and are not managing a home, one should be enough to cover your needs. Be sure to do a daily and weekly check in to make sure all transactions add up and are not repeated. We suggest you download your bank's mobile application to gain around the clock access to your finances with the click of a button.

Getting a second credit card might be a good idea if you do own a home and have expenses related to it. For this, it might be a good idea to do further research and really figure out your options because banks might not be offering the best product for you and your needs. If it is for your home and renovations are being done, consider signing up for a credit card from a place like the Home Depot. These stores often offer special discounts such as no interest for a certain amount of months and store points to be used with other purchases. Since home expenses often are not constant, or cheap, having two credit cards for the mentioned different purposes is recommended.

CONCLUSION

As a rollercoaster of a self-help guide, I hope to have informed and inspired you in any way possible on your journey to becoming a better you. Changing old habits, mindsets and ways of life is a hard route one must conquer on their quest to improve themselves. I hope this was the purpose of your readings when you picked up the text. While the end goal may have been to be in a better place financially, you must understand that you have to build a foundation before reaching your wealth goals.

Consider this concept when changing your mindset. You would certainly think that the stockbrokers on Wall Street seldom consider their mindset and mindfulness and manifestation when they are bringing in millions of billions of dollars every day. This may or may not be right. A lot of very successful people have claimed to have manifested their positions and seem to be people quite in touch with themselves even though at times they may not appear to be.

On your personal journey, consider the reasons for even picking up this book and your end goal. Are you someone who has always struggled to stay on top of debt, or are you just trying to become a first-time home owner? No matter the goal, the journey is still similar. Staying grounded and finding your true reasons for wanting to be successful and for wanting to be the best you that you can bear certainly the foundations of doing so. Saving money and investing money only become hard and time consuming if you deem them to be.

Putting in the time to learn new skills such as investing, or understanding how to better safely store your money through use of 401K or tax-free savings accounts are some ways you are already improving you. Putting in the time and effort and research now for you to live comfortably in a decade or so is a better bargain than most would consider.

You cannot teach an old dog new tricks they say and we strongly disagree. We think old dogs learn new tricks all the time and that is what must have kept them young all this time. In order to be different, to be better, you must consider all of your old and outdated habits and way of thinking. Ditch all that for new and improved habits and ones that truly are for building the better you. Think about parts of your life that you think could improve and brainstorm ways of doing so.

A lady who hates her body the way it is and wishes she could be thinner eats ice cream when she is stressed out. This lady sits down every day and wishes for a better body, and wonders why she does not have one yet. She is stressed often. She eats a gallon of ice cream but she still takes the stairs instead of the elevators at work. She thinks she put in enough effort. In this case, old habits are destructive and could not possibly produce an outcome for the desired future of being slimmer. Now, the lady has realized this. She has set up a punching bag in her basement and everytime she is mad, she punches the weighted bag that hangs sturdily from the ceiling. She eventually drops her ice cream routine to the point that it does not even cross her mind anymore. Now every time she's mad, all she thinks about is going home to punch her bag. She loses 60 pounds in the year and reaches for goal.

The takeaway from this example is the importance of being self-aware and making constant progress towards improvement. Changing one little aspect of her life that is not otherwise a big deal has allowed the lady to be the best her that she can be and through her confidence, she can now accomplish so much more. This is the example we would like to lead in our text and hope we have inspired you to do the same. No bad habit is too big or too small to break and slow progress is always better than no progress. Make your presence through your drive and discipline. Display and brag about your accomplishments in the spotlight.

In your many endeavors in life, one thing you should keep in mind from this book and being on the road to becoming financially literate and responsible and stable is the importance of decision making. Throughout this book it is discussed so many times and yet it really is not stressed enough. Every minor decision you make in your mundane daily life fits into a bigger puzzle piece at the end of the day that comes together to build a picture that is your future self. If you are determined to become a better version of yourself and to live the lifestyle that you want to have, consider any and all decisions you make moving forward.

Make better decisions than the ones you have made so far and make a conscious effort to do so. Changing your habits and realizing your full potential will open doors for you that your old self never thought possible. These behaviors will show themselves in financial forms too. From the way you earn money to the way you spend it. We hope you have picked up on some valuable lessons and ways to improve your daily life. We also hope to have stressed enough the importance of making changes to your life, no matter how big or how small. Creating that ripple effect and watching how it works out and celebrating your achievements are the best parts of evolving. You will notice the changes you have made before anyone else does and you can keep going knowing that as you go on, changes become more noticeable and people will begin to notice and congratulate you as time goes on. Who knows, you might even one day become an inspiration to some people like others have inspired you.

More than that, knowing you have the peace of mind to know you have worked for your money is a great feeling. Finally, being able to rest knowing that you have put in the work to be debt free while building your savings and ensuring a more comfortable future for yourself and your loved ones is one that is worth sacrificing for. Enjoying the time you are given now while preparing for a more relaxed and comfortable future in your retirement or even absence is the financial stability that you are searching for. Wealth does not mean having millions. Wealth is knowing that you are prepared for whatever comes next without drastically being affected. This is why organizing and anticipating are so important.

Financially literate people often know exactly where their hard-earned money is at all times. Spending and saving wise, your money should be kept track of even when you do not think it is necessary. All expenses and debits and credits should hold a place in your mind. This will keep you from paying any hidden fees or be ripped off in any way. It will also help you with a more conscious spending as time goes and you will also likely become a lot more aware of where your money is headed.

And so, be mindful and grounded in all that you do. Try to keep the exercises in mind and practice them as you need. Keep in mind decisions are what makes your life the way that it is and you are one good or bad decision away from a better or a worse lifestyle than you have. And if your process takes longer, be at peace knowing that you are on your way. Do not let anything deter you from the peace of mind and winning mindset we have created. Wealth is in the mind and as long as you believe it, you can achieve it.

REFERENCES

Explained: The Stock Market. (2020). *YouTube.*

https://www.youtube.com/watch?v=ZCFkWDdmXG8
HYPERLINK
"https://www.youtube.com/watch?v=ZCFkWDdmXG8
&ab_channel=Netflix"& HYPERLINK
"https://www.youtube.com/watch?v=ZCFkWDdmXG8
&ab_channel=Netflix"ab_channel=Netflix.

Analytics, Neris. "Free Personality Test." *16Personalities*. Web. 20
May 2021.

Made in the USA
Middletown, DE
22 July 2021